Walter & Emma Smith

Their Family's Story in Their Own Words

John M. Smith, *Editor*

BALBOA.PRESS
A DIVISION OF HAY HOUSE

Balboa Press books may be ordered through booksellers or by contacting:

Balboa Press
A Division of Hay House
1663 Liberty Drive
Bloomington, IN 47403
www.balboapress.com
844-682-1282

Because of the dynamic nature of the Internet, any web addresses or links contained in this book may have changed since publication and may no longer be valid. The views expressed in this work are solely those of the author and do not necessarily reflect the views of the publisher, and the publisher hereby disclaims any responsibility for them.

The author of this book does not dispense medical advice or prescribe the use of any technique as a form of treatment for physical, emotional, or medical problems without the advice of a physician, either directly or indirectly. The intent of the author is only to offer information of a general nature to help you in your quest for emotional and spiritual well-being. In the event you use any of the information in this book for yourself, which is your constitutional right, the author and the publisher assume no responsibility for your actions.

Any people depicted in stock imagery provided by Getty Images are models, and such images are being used for illustrative purposes only. Certain stock imagery © Getty Images.

Print information available on the last page.

ISBN: 978-1-9822-5252-6 (sc)
ISBN: 978-1-9822-5253-3 (e)

Balboa Press rev. date: 09/09/2020

Acknowledgements

For their assistance and permission to use their likeness, letters, and/ or copyrighted material, I would like to thank Walter & Emma Smith, their children, Emma's brothers Carl & Charles Lutes, the Christopher Progress, Christopherian, Tim Price and his online blog: *Turning Out the Lights at Epworth Camp*, Clay County Advocate-Press, Southern Illinois Methodist Bulletin, Lawrenceville Daily Record, Wayne County Press, Mt. Vernon Register News, Albion Journal Register, and The Southern Illinoisan newspaper.

Contents

Acknowledgements v

Introduction ix

Growing Up in Christopher 1

The Lutes Family 19

The Duckworth Family 41

Walter's Childhood 45

Reflections on Commuting to College 49

My College Years 57

Courtship & Marriage 59

Early Married Life 63

Memories of Early Days at Epworth Camp 69

Europe and the Holy Land 77

Flora, Illinois 111

Missionary Letters from the Far East 113

Other Places Where We Have Lived 179

Walter's Illness & Widowhood 207

Events of Interest 219

Thoughts on Growing Older 225

Her Favorites 227

Benedictions 231

The Mystery of Angels by Walter 233

Epilogue 241

Introduction

The Roaring 20's, the Great Depression, World War II, the Korean Conflict, the Cold War, and the turbulent times during the 1960's are historic events for most of us. All these were part of daily life for Walter Smith and Emma Lutes as they grew up when automobiles, airplanes, and trains were a thing of awe and wonder for poor, hard working people. Life at home was simple as they were devoid of the "luxuries" of a radio, more than one electric light in the house, and lack of indoor plumbing.

Hard play, daily chores, and religion were their major influences. Playing and doing chores around the house all week in their bare feet, the children dressed in their finest clothes and shoes on Sundays and trudged to their church of choice for religious training and services. Sundays at church would play a major role in Walter and Emma's personal development and eventually their lives together. It set the background for living their lives, honoring and serving our creator, and raising their family.

Born in 1915, Walter was the son of a Methodist minister. He learned first-hand the trials and triumphs of ministering to the flock. He learned how to sow the seeds of the teachings of the Bible and reap the rewards of religious conversion of others. He was determined to learn as much as possible about his religion, perhaps even teach it to others. It served him well as he obtained his bachelor and master's degrees in education and religion, the most education of anyone in his family. Graduating from Garrett Seminary in 1946, he became an ordained minister and earned an honorary doctorate degree in religion from McKendree College in 1954.

Emma, born in 1921, was the daughter of a religious mother and carefree father. Emma embraced the church at a young age and wanted to raise her family with her own religious zeal. She was also determined to be educated and was the first in her family to graduate from high school and attend college, earning a teaching certificate. It was this faith and desire for further education that brought them together on the campus of Southern Illinois Normal University in 1939.

This is their story, most of which is edited from memoirs, letters, and other documents written mostly by them. Their original letters and accounts were written in random order and some attempt was made to place them in chronological order. Therefore, some editing was done to allow their writings to flow together in a logical, story-telling manner, and edited for the sake of clarity, spelling, and grammar.

Although many of Walter and Emma's letters and writings were faithfully kept, there may be periods of time for which the written documents do not account. Information about these periods has been added by their children, relatives, friends, and newspaper accounts in order to give the family life of Walter and Emma a more complete picture.

Formatting for this document is as follows: Walter and Emma's written memoirs are noted as written by them and are in <u>block paragraphs</u>, letters to and from them are presented in *italics*, their travel itineraries and this editor's comments are preceded with the phrase "<u>Editor's note</u>" and is indented or "<u>ed. note</u>" and if there is more than one paragraph then there is an "###" at the end, and newspaper articles are preceded by the <u>name of the publication</u>.

The following are clarifications of the names within this document; Charles W. Lutes (Emma's father) was called "Charlie," his son Charles was called "Charles" or "Peanut," Charles R. Smith was called "Bud" or "Buddy" as a child then was referred to as "Charlie" as an adult, and John Smith was called "Mark" as a child, "John Mark" as an adolescent, and "John" as an adult. Southern Illinois University Carbondale was originally named Southern Illinois Normal University or SINU ("normal" was a state designation for a college that primarily trained school teachers) and later just Southern Illinois University or SIU.

Acknowledgements are hereby given to my siblings and uncles for their contributions and anecdotes that add liveliness, meaning, and alternative perspectives to this family's story.

Be aware that some of the references and words herein are from a time period when the term "politically correct" was not used or even known as a concept. Please forgive any of these transgressions.

As a final comment, transcribing these documents has been very insightful, rewarding, and inspiring. One word of caution is that these writings may cause the reader to smile, occasionally laugh, evoke memories, or even cause the dreaded "misty eyes" syndrome.

Enjoy!

Respectfully,
John M. Smith, child #4

Christopher Progress Newspaper

CHRISTOPHER, January 1921 -- At 11 o'clock last Sunday night the stork visited the home of Constable C. W. Lutes, 512 South Emma Street and presented him with a fine nine and three-quarters pound baby girl.

Mr. Lutes was all smiles Monday morning and although he preferred a boy, he was as proud as he could be of his little daughter. Both mother and baby are doing fine.

The Progress congratulates Mr. and Mrs. Lutes.

Emma Lutes, 1921

###

Growing Up In Christopher, Illinois by Emma

I don't remember being in my mother's womb, being born at home in January 1921, or losing our house, car, and piano during my early years. I don't remember being ill at all as mom must have made it easy for us.

I do remember living on South Emma Street in Christopher and playing house with my sister Laura, under the round, dark dining room table covered with a lace cloth that dropped down to the floor.

I remember giving my doll a bath in the rain barrel that sat under the down spout from our roof. The doll was ruined since it was made of paper. I remember going with my dad who was fire chief to see the fire wagon pulled by horses named Dan and Bob.

When I was born on the south side of Christopher, mom (Bessie Duckworth Lutes) and dad (Charles W. Lutes) bought the house that dad's nephew, Russell owned. The nephew went to California. So dad and mom about that time got married and bought that house on South Emma Street. When I was about five, we moved to the north side of Christopher.

My favorite pet was a large Shepherd and Collie-mix dog named "Shep" and how could I forget the hot summer dad sheared him of his lovely, reddish brown hair. He then looked like a wolf.

I can't remember being afraid in storms, I must have felt safe. We didn't have much of this world's goods, but we always felt loved. That was more important anyway.

It was hot in the summer and cold in the winter, but I don't remember suffering too much. We had fans and sat out under the trees feeling the breeze when it was too hot in the house -- of course, mother went inside to fix the meals. I remember sleeping on the porch or the floor many times in summer. We had goose down pillows and covers in the winter.

When we were small, I remember six-button shoes. We used button hooks to fasten and unfasten them.

I remember, except for school and church, the accepted heat was pot belly stoves fired by coal, which was plentiful because we lived over mines of it. Mother was of English descent and when she could find one, we had a cooked goose for Christmas dinner. She always kept the down feathers from them to make our pillows. Our couches and chairs were filled with horsehair instead of the fillings of today. It was bouncy, but came back into place when we arose. I can't remember what the contents of mattresses were made of, only that they were different from today's mattresses.

Christopher was a town, I would guess like very many others in the area. It was a mining town. Many people from Europe had come over here to live in Christopher. I remember that the women were especially, especially neat. They cleaned their house every day. I couldn't imagine doing that today, still can't.

Many of the residents of Christopher came from Europe: Italy, Slavic counties, Russia, Germany, and worked in the coal mines. We were a very diverse community. At one time we lived on what was called "dago hill," a nickname for Italians. Each area in Christopher had such a nickname.

They tended to live, as people do, in the part of the town where the people who came from their country lived. So, we had a "bob" hill and a "dago" hill. It was just a normal word, not a bad word. I remember a Russian family lived there. So, they came from all parts of Europe and were miners or in the mining business.

Some of them could speak the language of their parents. Their parents spoke their foreign language and had not learned too much English. But, I remember that the children wanted to get away from the foreign language and be more American almost to the point of being "snobs."

When mom taught first grade, she said that three-fourths of them couldn't speak English at all. The others interpreted for her. It didn't take long for them to learn English when they were around the other kids. But, they spoke their parent's language at home.

I remember mom making her own soaps with strange ingredients. She took ashes, fat, shoot and made big ugly looking bars. She had little bits of lye in it, which may have been found naturally in the ashes. It was vile. It burned your skin and stunk. I wanted nothing to do with it.

If we had a toothbrush, we wash our teeth with salt or soap. Salt was gritty and probably not good for your teeth. You didn't do that anymore than you had to. But you know we were happy.

In the winter we would wake up in the morning. We would grab our clothes and go back to bed to put them on because it was warmer in bed than in the room. I remember it would freeze a little in the house if there was any liquid about on some bad nights. We slept in long johns, no pajamas back then. We had a clean pair each Sunday and by Saturday we reeked. Saturday night we had a metal bath tub bath and started the new week clean. I remember when I taught school in the country those kids did the same thing. By Friday, that school really stunk. Those were the good old days.

We wore cotton socks. I certainly didn't have name brand shoes or clothes. I don't know how my parents afforded to clothe all of us. Mother made most of our dresses. We didn't wear sports clothing.

Growing Up in Christopher
By Emma

When I was in Junior High my friend Anna and I were brave enough to wear a sailor suit and anklets in summer, and in the winter some jodhpurs, navy blue and made of corduroy (ed. note: jodhpurs are full-length trousers worn for horseback riding, that are close-fitting below the knee, and have reinforced patches on the inside of the leg.) She probably bought mine so she felt secure wearing hers. We didn't wear slacks in those days, just dresses. Also, I remember when we went to school they wouldn't let you in until the first bell.

Mother had taught in the Christopher school system for eight years, so she taught me to read before I went to school. As there was no kindergarten, I went to first grade on the south side of town while I was just five years old, not turning six until January. The girls lined up to go in the school by one door and the boys by another.

Classes in school were not large like they are today. I was not aware of the size. If I remember correctly, there would be around 15 maybe 20 kids in a class. I remember we walked to school; everyone had to walk because nobody, very few had cars. We had to stay on the school grounds until school started and sometimes we were pretty cold by the time we got to go inside. I nearly froze to death because we also had to walk to school in the cold.

The first thing we usually did was sing together. I remember our principal loved to sing and he'd have us sing all kinds of songs. Then we would go to our classrooms. We'd bring our lunches if we lived too far away to walk home, especially if the weather was bad. They were kind of pitiful compared to today's lunches, but they filled us up. We started school at nine and got out at four.

I've seen a lot of change in my lifetime. When we started school in the fall, a lot of children came barefoot, with no shoes. They saved their shoes for winter. I remember going to a friend's house and the floor was dirt. I don't think people were any unhappier than they are now. They were just glad to get whatever they could get.

I remember when in the third grade the teacher decided to put on a play. I wanted so badly to be in it, but not everyone could. I was not chosen. It broke my heart. Later in the year she had another and those of us who were not in the first one were in it. I have never wanted to be in a play since. It wasn't my "thing," but I still remember the heart break of the first rejection.

We went to the sixth grade in one school. For the seventh and eighth grades, we had to go across town. I had a real good eighth grade English teacher. She stood for no non-sense and we had to learn how to speak good English.

I remember walking to school and we'd go by a tree that had persimmons. We would pick up the persimmons and eat them. We'd open them up and the seed looked like spoons. There were simple pleasures in those days.

We moved regularly, but I lived the rest of my childhood days in Christopher on the north or west side of town. My twin brothers, Carl and Charles, were born on Cherry Street six years after I entered the world and my brother Jim when I was ten (ed. note: she was about 18 months old and too young to remember when her sister Laura was born.) The doctors in those days came to the homes for births as well as illnesses.

When the Great Depression came, everyone lost what they had and everyone was poor it seemed. All of our lights came from bulbs hanging from covered electrical wires attached to the ceiling. We pulled a chain in order to turn them on and off. We didn't have any lamps or plug-in appliances.

I remember when we lived on Cherry Street, where Carl and Charles were born, and the kids across the street, the Kauzlarich boys, made a miniature golf course in the vacant lot next door. They charged one penny to play the course, it had several holes. Each hole was a different kind; one sent the ball through a tunnel, probably a tomato juice can or a 5 pound wooden cheese box, painted a bright color. Another hole would send the ball around an obstacle; another would be decorated with stones to go over or through two pillars made of two glass bottles. It took a lot of imagination and we kids of the neighborhood thought it was wonderful and often nagged our parents for pennies or used our small allowances to pay the golf course fee. One day the boys were to be away and asked me to be in charge. I felt really important collecting the pennies. Pennies meant something in those days.

I remember my mother cooking lots of potatoes, apples, and peaches in season and canning them -- the over ripes (ed. note: over ripe fruit) were cheap. I guess I got my love to cook with onions from mother. Mother cooked on a coal fueled kitchen stove. I will never understand how she could bake pies on it. Mine are not good even when cooked with an electric oven. Many breakfasts were biscuits and gravy, bacon and eggs, sausage, etc. In the winter it was usually oatmeal. Later we started using cereals.

Dad always had a big garden. He was a good gardener. We canned vegetables and root vegetables -- carrots, beets, garlic, turnips, potatoes, rutabaga, onions and sweet potatoes -- and they were put down into a root cellar, below ground, to keep until we needed them. We had lots of turnips in season -- needless to say it was not our favorite food back then. Milk, bread, and eggs were staples. Bananas, the over ripes, were 25 cents per peck sock. We loved banana pudding and pies. Mom made a lot of jellies and jams, and the bakery sold "day old bread" at a reduced price. We couldn't afford to eat out and there were practically no restaurants -- especially for the common fellas. Meat was a delicacy, we loved it and when we had it we had lots of roasts and fried chicken on Sundays.

I remember spring cleaning at everyone's house. The sturdy people would take the rug out to the clothesline, hang it over the line, and we would all take turns beating the dust out of it with a rug beater very similar to a tennis racquet. This happened after the stove was taken down and the pipes cleaned of soot. Windows and curtains were washed and many times the room was repapered. Beds were torn apart and everything washed and aired. Coal stoves made everything dirty and everything had to be cleaned in the only way we could.

I remember that some of the old regal houses when I was a child were the same architecture as the newest houses are today. Most of the houses in our little mining town were small modest houses.

I remember that in the evenings the neighborhood kids came together and played "hide and seek" until our mothers called us in at dark. We did not have street lights to play under. I didn't play much with dolls. We didn't have store bought toys, except for wagons and skates. We made scooters from discarded skates, not the shoe-type. It was fun to squash a tin can and walk on them while stuck to our shoes.

Our games were jacks, jump rope while chanting poems as we jumped sometimes two people together, and hop scotch on marked up sidewalks. I'm not sure where the chalk came from to mark up the sidewalks. I hope not from school.

I remember sitting on the lawn on a blanket while dad mowed the yard and as he came near I inadvertently laid out my hand and the mower clipped it a little. Everyone made a big fuss over me. The sore it made no longer shows through my wrinkles these days.

I remember "Shep," my first dog. I haven't had many. It was a German shepherd mixed with Collie. I got it as a pup, but it grew quickly into a large dog and followed Laura and me everywhere. I guess you could say that it was our protector, though there wasn't much need of protection in those days.

I remember one hot summer dad decided that Shep needed to have less thick long hair on his body. Dad shaved the whole dog of his long thick hair like he would a sheep. We were horrified as poor Shep looked so awful, like a skinned animal. By winter all his hair grew back and he looked like his old rust-colored self.

We had no car, so I walked wherever I went, school, church, grocery store in all kinds of weather. I grew up in the days of few cars, everyone walked. There were no buses to and from school or the store or drug store or any place else. Because we had to walk so much, I am able to still get around so well at my age of almost 90.

Emma, Laura & Shep, ca 1925

I will never forget the beginning of oleo margarine. When we could afford it we had butter, and then on the market appeared a white lard-like substance with an orange capsule in the package. The idea was to open the capsule onto the white mass and mix it, usually with our hands for the warmth of our hands mixed it best, until it was a nice yellow color.

I usually got this job and I hated it. I can still feel that gooey substance on my hands today. This method of mixture continued for several years until the manufacturers decided to mix it themselves with machines.

I remember the first time I saw time-lapse photography. It was of a rose. It was the most beautiful thing I had ever seen. Today that seems simple as all the new technology has taken us into a world I cannot understand. I remember that my poor grandmother could hardly accept the world moving by car instead of horse power.

And, airplanes! Whenever one flew over our house we all ran out to watch and listen to it pass over. They were so rare that it was quite a treat to see them.

I remember an incident from my childhood. It was a time during the depression and we had hit an especially low place financially. For my school lunch, mother sliced a turnip and put it between slices of bread. It was weird, but nourishing. I was not fond of turnips then, but I am today.

I remember that most of us had no telephone. When we did get one, it was a party line, that is, 3 or 4 families used the same telephone line. We could all listen in on the community gossip. Often if there was an emergency we had to ask the person talking on the line to "please hang up so we could get through" to our doctor or whoever we needed to contact.

We finally got a radio and enjoyed listening to it as a family. I remember Saturday nights gathering around to hear a continuing mystery called, "The Squeaking Door." Of course westerns, music, and Gospel were plentiful.

I read a lot and couldn't put a book down until it was finished. I still have this habit. Some of my favorites were "Lassie," "The Last of the Mohicans," and later "Jane Eyre."

At one of our houses we had a well and drew water in a bucket. We had an outhouse where dad grew tall sunflowers to cover it. Outhouses were the bathroom of the time. Someone was hired to regularly go around town to clean the outhouses and carry away the contents. We called these wagons pulled by horses a honey bucket. I can almost smell them today. The rest of the houses where we lived had indoor plumbing.

Growing Up in Christopher
By Emma

We always had electricity, but electric ice boxes were rare, so an ice truck came by every day with 50 or 100 pound blocks of ice. The delivery boy brought them in and placed them in our ice chest. Some of the ice chests were very nice pieces of furniture.

When twins Carl and Charles were small, mother tried to keep them dressed alike. They were so different in looks and disposition, likes and dislikes, that they soon changed how they dressed.

Our twin brothers, younger than Laura and I by six years, were big pests. They conspired with each other to spy on us, make fun of our boyfriends, put frogs down our dresses so they jumped around on our backs just above our belts, and were in general nuisances to us young ladies. Our younger brother, Jim, often joined in. Three against one or two of us!

Jim came along late in mother and dad's life. He loved to try to keep up with his older brothers. They wouldn't let him go along with them so he followed them at a distance. When they were so far from home that they couldn't send him home alone, he presented himself and they had to let him "tag along."

The three of them had lots of fun. Whatever project one couldn't think up, the other could. They "egged" each other on and did many fun things they shouldn't have done, pranks mostly. They often "snickered" about some of their pranks as they get older.

Occasionally, mother would let Laura and I ride a small railcar that travelled from Christopher to Sesser and back. It was called the "Dinky." We went to Sesser to visit my aunt and uncle, Floy and Ralph Duckworth and their two daughters Vivian and Dorothy. They lived on a farm north of Sesser and we walked from the station to their house.

They had pigs, horses, and cows and the "always under foot" chickens, with of course the "king" rooster who crowed at daybreak. Eggs were gathered morning and night. We pushed the cackling hens out of the nest and gathered the eggs in a basket.

It was quite an experience as we went out to the pasture with our cousins, all of us barefoot, to bring home the cows from the pastures each evening. After the cows were milked, Aunt Floy let the milk sit overnight in a crock, the cream would rise to the top. She dipped it off and churned it -- this made the butter. If the milk soured, as there was no electricity on the farm, there was cottage cheese to eat.

In the fall, they invited us to come for the harvest season. This was quite an event in our lives. All of the farmers would help each other harvest the wheat. They went from farm to farm with whatever machinery they had and cooperated in the work.

The ladies fixed the meal for the "harvest hands." It was quite a meal, usually vegetables from the garden as by then they were plentiful, and fried chicken was heaped high on the platter. What I remember most is the banana pudding. The pudding itself was made from the eggs and milk that were plentiful in very large vats, then put together with graham crackers and bananas. I loved these meals.

Screen doors were essential as flies and other insects were prevalent. The use of DDT has eliminated most of them today (ed. note: the use of DDT, a potent substance used to kill insects, was used extensively by 1945 and then banned as a cancer-causing poison by the USDA in 1972.)

My grandmother Duckworth, the only one I knew, lived on the family farm with mom's younger sister Cora until Cora got married; I was about ten or eleven. When Aunt Cora got married to Mr. Warren, grandma broke up housekeeping and rented her farm to Uncle Hershel. I think Hershel had been farming for her anyway. And then he moved out onto the farm. I don't know how long he lived there, but he lived there a while.

Grandma then started living with each of her children; Ralph, Raleigh, and mom took turns having her stay at their houses. When she moved to our house we had just four rooms and Laura and I gave up our room so she could have it for herself when she came to live permanently with us.

It was quite a sacrifice as we lived in a four room house at the time. Mom and dad and the three boys shared a very large bedroom. The boys slept together. My grandmother Duckworth had her own room and Laura and I slept on the pull out couch in the living room. We all ate at the large round table in the kitchen.

When grandmother Duckworth left her farmhouse near Akin, she brought with her beautiful cut and pressed glass items. There were two or three barrels full. All of the relatives were welcome to take what they wanted. I received a cake-sized square plate that sat up on a stem. The corner lips of the plate turned down. The pattern was Pricilla. I showcased it on my dining room table after I got married.

Emma Duckworth, circa 1931

She also brought with her several items, including a large wooden, four post bed, dresser, trunk full of treasures, and an armoire that went almost to the ceiling. I don't know what happened to them when she died.

She lived with us, I can't remember, maybe a couple of years and died there. They had the funeral in Christopher, as I remember, at the funeral home. I think grandmother Duckworth got sick, sick in bed for a while. As a child, I don't remember too much about it. They took her to the funeral home and brought her back to our house. They took the bed out and that was where she lay for the viewing.

I can't remember if the funeral service was at our house or the funeral home, but then they took her out and buried her in the cemetery at Knob Prairie beside her husband.

Grandmother Duckworth was about 78 when she passed. She was not a very big lady. Of course in those days people didn't live as long. Grandpa Duckworth was in his fifties when he passed, so was great grandpa Smith. In those days the men were out in the fields and often got sick.

I remember one time when Aunt Cora came by she gave her some candy that grandma hid in the closet; we kids got into it and eat some of the candy.

Uncle Raleigh and his family came to visit us every once in a while and stayed the day. We always enjoyed that because we children could get together and play for the day.

I remember they had the Duckworth Reunion at the Benton Lake. Mom always went. They would come by and get grandma and us. While she was at the picnic reunion she would watch the children so all the adults could go swimming. I remember her telling that she enjoyed it, because she enjoyed children.

When Aunt Cora and her husband worked, in a penitentiary I think, they were the ones who made grandpa and grandma Duckworth's cemetery stones. They are same stones that are there today.

I have no recollection of grandma talking about her parents, at all. I don't remember her husband, at all. And, as a child, I wasn't really that interested. She was not very outgoing. She was not talkative and did not talk about her life as a child. She was a little on the bashful order. She spoke good American English as it was her grandfather that came from England. Where he lived or how he lived I have no recollection of her talking about it.

She gave me a quilt because I was her namesake. I was just seven, and at seven who cares about an old quilt. Today, I would treasure it.

My best friend through grade and high school was Anna. Her parents owned a grocery store and she could have anything she wanted out of that store. She had more spending money than I and was very generous to share with me. It was fun to pick out the penny candy from each of the candy bins. Pickles, large dill ones, were in a barrel and for a nickel could be eaten. I liked pickles even as a child, but nickels were scarce. Anna had a bicycle. We couldn't afford one. My friend generously shared her bike. We spent every weekend washing that bike, then using Vaseline to shine the spokes. It was fun work.

Guess where she "lived?" at our house almost all of the time. At her house they ate all kinds of meats that we didn't have. But what they didn't have was a family closeness like we had. We were her family. When she got married, she must have envisioned having a ton of children. She couldn't have children so they had to adopt two. She probably spoiled them.

Growing Up in Christopher
By Emma

Anna's parents often spoke in their native language when they didn't want us kids to know what they were saying. They were from the Czechoslovakian region of Europe. Anna knew enough of it to understand, but she wanted to be American and didn't want anything to do with the old language. Many kids in Christopher were like that at the time.

I remember when people in the store would speak in a Czechoslovakian language or something close to it so that Anna's parents could understand them. That's how their customers communicated when in the store and didn't speak English.

My Junior High School was across town. With no family car, we walked to school, home for lunch and back, and then home after school. My twin brothers went there for kindergarten, which the town had just started. Needless to say, when the weather became too severe, my brothers had to drop out of school.

I remember Isaac Walton's pond and "pig" pond where we could swim. My siblings, Laura, Carl, Charles, and Jim walked two miles to a mine pit filled with rain water in order to swim. They then walked the two miles home. I refused to get all sweaty walking to and from there. I didn't want to learn to swim badly enough to do this; hence, I never learned to swim and frankly didn't miss it. Subsequently, I made sure all of my children had swimming lessons from the Red Cross. One of them even grew up and gave Red Cross swimming lessons to other children.

My sister Laura was always so well coordinated that she did all sports well. She skated at the roller rink so well that all of the boys wanted to skate with her. I was so klutzy that they only skated with me to be polite. Laura danced, too. She was good at the "Charleston." I never learned to dance at all.

One thing that my sister Laura was poor at was taking care of her clothes. She didn't want to bother. We didn't have a lot of "good" clothes. Mother made most of our clothes. One time dad bought each of us a new dress. Laura's was usually draped on the floor. I took pride in mine and kept it carefully hanging. We were about the same size. Needless to say, one evening Laura had a date, her dress was all wrinkled, so she wore mine without asking. I haven't forgiven her yet for that.

I remember at least one time when Laura's friend got his dad's car and came to pick her up and as they left, my brothers threw rotten tomatoes at the car. He had just had the car washed for his date.

The church near Akin, where mother grew up, held a homecoming picnic each year. One year mother wanted us all to go, so dad rented a truck. We all piled in with our picnic lunch and went to Benton on decent roads. It had rained and when we got on the country roads to Akin, it became treacherous. Finally, the truck got stuck on the muddy road and we almost burned up the motor trying to get out of the muck. We turned around and ate our picnic lunch at home. All of us were disappointed.

As a teenager, we still walked a lot as did most of the residents, especially children and youth. We walked and talked. Maybe that is why I'm so good at it now. Our boyfriends walked to our houses even if they were from nearby villages. They "hitched" a ride into town and back to their home. We went to a movie, or church, or just walked and talked and maybe grabbed a "Maid Rite" (ed. note: a local restaurant that cooks hamburger meat and places it loosely on a bun) and a soft drink. Occasionally, a boy's father allowed him to drive his car and at least three couples piled in just to ride around. I assume the boys pitched in on the gas. It was fun to walk downtown in the evening and see and talk to others down there. The country folk would come into town, park their cars, and watch people go by. That's the way it was!

People living in the country had cars. They came into the towns on Saturday evenings. They did a lot of business, but their entertainment was watching the people go by. The "city" people's entertainment was to meet each other downtown and if we had the money, get a lemon or cherry coke at the drug store. The glassful was only a nickel and the "soda jerk" was usually a popular kid from school. Ice cream cones, three dips for a nickel, were also popular.

We all wore dresses in those days, as culottes and jeans were not worn. Many of them had to be ironed. I guess that is when I learned the art. I put it to good use when I had my big family and even ironed sheets. One day I counted 35 shirts and blouses, besides dresses. It took me most of two days.

High school, I thought, was great. I didn't know much about the sports that everybody was raving about, but I would watch them. I attended most of the football games, mostly because of the crowd as the game meant little to me. It still doesn't. I didn't know what was happening when they were tackling each other on the football field. One of my friends had made up yells (ed. note: coordinated cheers) and we all participated in that.

I joined several clubs in high school. I had nothing to do at home so I could stay for the meetings after school. It served as a way for us to socialize. I remember being in the Glee Club and coming to Carbondale for a Glee Club chorus. We sang "Whispering Hope" as a group of many clubs. It was a great experience for me. I have always loved music.

In high school, I dated a guy named Todd Taylor from Valier, just three miles away. Many of the boys came to Christopher to see girls. Laura dated several fellows from there. They had their own high school back then. Todd played tuba in the high school band. We attended high school events and went to church together, though his mother was a staunch Southern Baptist and thought I might "contaminate" her son with my staunch Methodism. Our favorite place was to go to the Maid Rite restaurant, which still exists. It was one of the first fast food places. We walked most places we went as very few people could afford cars.

I remember one Christmas, a lady from Valier crocheted lovely paisley sweaters and all the guys bought one as a gift for their girlfriends. Todd wanted to get me one and it took a lot of persuading mother to let me accept it. Boys weren't supposed to buy clothes for girls, at least in her eyes.

I remember taking two years of Latin. We never intended to speak or write it, but it was great to improve our English for so many words are based on Latin words and phrases.

Laura skipped school whenever she could. To my sister Laura, school was just a place to have fun. She was smart enough, but she just didn't want to learn, especially from reading books. I don't know if she didn't read well or what. I enjoyed school, so I loved to go, but I have never been as observant as Laura was. She really never enjoyed studying after her third year of high school. Mom expected us to go to school.

Laura decided "she had had it" so she didn't return for her last year of school. Mom, with her rare insight into human personalities, decided that if Laura wasn't going to school, she could cook and do the dishes, no dishwashers in those days, and clean house. Her skipping school lasted about two days. Laura decided that school wasn't so bad after all and finished high school.

For my last year in high school, the principal asked me if I would keep the attendance records for the school. I worked in the office all of that year. It provided WPA monies for my family (ed. note: the WPA was a work program during the Great Depression.) All of the teachers would send in the attendance records, and for the whole year I would put lines across the morning or afternoon when the kids were absent. That's the way they figured out who came to school and who didn't. Of course, that's the way the State paid the school, according to attendance. I enjoyed the work, but since I worked after school, I missed school activities. I especially missed Glee Club where I sang second soprano.

Christopher High School Yearbook

CHRISTOPHERIAN, 1935 -- The Christopher High School was organized in the fall of 1909. The course of study consisted of two years work. On April 11, 1911, occurred the first graduating exercises of the high school with three students.

In 1917, four years' work was offered. The school was placed on the list of accredited high schools by the state. The course of study was the same as offered in some of the best high schools in Southern Illinois. Also, the Christopherian was published for the first time in 1917.

In 1919, the graduating class numbered five. Up to this time the high school occupied a few rooms in the Franklin School. The American Legion Hall was used for a gym for practicing basketball. In 1921, a new gym was built and known as the Chevrolet garage. The first football team was organized, but there was much to learn about the game to offer much competition to experienced teams, making improvement over the first few years to win three of nine games.

In 1922, the community voted to create a community high school known as district number 38. In the fall, a site was chosen to build the first high school building. By 1924 the graduating class numbered twenty-three. The new building would house domestic science, well-equipped laboratories, and a gymnasium. The year of 1933 showed a marked increase in attendance with an enrollment of 480 students.

Christopher High School Yearbook

CHRISTOPHERIAN, 1938 -- Emma Lutes, nickname "Spankie" (ed. note: a name given to her by her friend Anna), participated in music, girl's athletics, home economics club, Hi-Tri, and Latin Club. She leaves her "giggles" to June Mackey. Would you guess...Emma Lutes' Chief Characteristic -- Turbulence, Favorite Saying -- "Nooooo?" Hangout -- Home (?), Her Future -- Office girl, and Hobby -- Doing nothing.

Seniors' legacy: "Our Record Here...Four years ago, we started out as the largest freshman class in the history of the Christopher Community High School, and now we are ending by having the largest senior class with an enrollment of ninety-six."

Emma's yearbook was inscribed by Anna as follows: "Dearest Emma, from the fifth grade on and through High School we have been friends to our senior years -- may our friendship last on into the future although we have been drifting apart. I hope not in thoughts. I shall never forget our walks 'up the corner' and talks. In many ways those years have helped me more then you will ever know. You know my best wishes for luck, success, and happiness are with you always. Love, Anna"

Letter to Carl Lutes from Emma

Mr. Carl Lutes
333 W. 56th Street,
Apt. 8M
New York, New York
November 3, 1997

Dear Carl,

Charlie & Bessie Lutes, circa 1950

I've written a bio of mom and dad, our children are asking us each to do this and eventually of our own remembrances of our own lives. I'm finally starting this process. Will you look it over, reword, rewrite and add your remembrances to it? I would not even mind if you typed it up so it could be photo copied, but that isn't necessary.

Eventually we must do one of Jim, but I'm not ready as yet. I'd like to question him. Dad talked a lot to him. I'd appreciate your thinking on your life, but one thing at a time.

Lillian called after you contacted her the other day. She was surprised that you and Jim had bonded so. Isn't it strange that she didn't see that?

I've needed addresses of our kids. They had sent a Harvest Basket of flowers for the funeral.

I haven't seen or heard from Laura. We will get together before we go south, whenever that will be.

I go back to the doctor on Monday and will delay sending this letter until I do. If it doesn't suit me, there is a retina clinic at Barnes. My eye is better, but how long must I endure?

We have most of our outside work done for the fall. It has turned frosty here (ed. note: the letter appeared to be completed after the visit to the doctor that was mentioned above.)

*I was at the other eye doctor this morning. He is encouraged.
The surgery is perfect; it healed 80% of the blister. He assures
me of 20/20 vision in that eye. I can get glasses in 3-4 weeks,
see him again December 1, and go off south. We'll do the other
eye in the spring. Patience is not my best quality.*

Love, Emma and Walter

Bessie Duckworth Lutes by Emma

Bessie was born in Williamson County, Illinois in April 1889 to William and Emma Alston Duckworth. She had three sisters and four brothers. She was the sixth child. Her parents had a farm near Colp, Illinois on the Big Muddy River near Big Bend. Their house was the first one in that area made from milled lumber "slats." All the other houses were log cabins. Besides farming, her father delivered the US Mail using his horse and wagon, delivering the mail once each week from Carterville to Colp.

When Bessie was about age 13, the "Number 9" coal company bought the Duckworth farm in Williamson County and the family moved to a farm between Benton and Thompsonville in Franklin County, near the village of Akin. Bessie lived on this farm until she was grown.

The first time she saw a car was when the doctor from Thompsonville drove his red car by her. About the same period of time, another car passed her church during worship services and the entire congregation stood quietly and gazed out the church windows until it passed and then sat down again and resumed worship. These experiences made quite an impression on her.

At age 21, Bessie taught a summer school session on the farm. Later, the Superintendent of Schools in Franklin County persuaded Bessie to take the "Teachers Exam" and teach in a country school. She taught for one year there and had nine students. She lived with the Superintendent and his wife and drove a horse and buggy to school each day. The next year that school was torn down to make way for a lake.

At that time, teachers had to take a course of study each year and monthly came together to discuss one of the books required for them to read. Once each year there was a county teacher's meeting where a professional speaker would lecture. Occasionally teachers were required to take a class at Southern Illinois Normal University in Carbondale. Bessie took two classes at SINU and received her teacher's certificate. The requirements were not too strict, but this was quite a step for a shy farm girl.

At age 23, she was hired to teach at Franklin School in Christopher, Illinois where she taught first or second grades for the next eight years. Bessie had about 30-50 pupils each term. Many of the children were first generation Americans and many could not speak English as their family spoke the native language at home. Their parents were immigrants from Europe and came here to work in the coal mines. Some of her pupils who could speak both languages helped her interpret with the ones that didn't know English. She often talked of a set of twins who cried most of the time because the school was so foreign to them. One of them later became the Latin teacher at the Christopher High School and was my Latin teacher, Ms. Anita Oberto.

While Bessie taught in Christopher, she lived with Dr. Brayfield and his wife. In those days there was no place to "board" except in private homes. Bessie and Mrs. Brayfield became good friends. The Brayfields were Methodists, so Bessie went with them to church, and later joined.

Charlie Lutes had a brother, John, who had moved to Christopher from West Virginia and was the building contractor for the Methodist Church. Charlie also moved to Christopher to help with the construction about 1919. Charlie and Bessie met there and after a romance, they were married in March 1920. John's wife, Levina, was Bessie's matron of honor. John and Levina moved to California in 1922.

Charlie and Bessie bought a house on North Emma Street in Christopher. They later lost it as did many others during the Great Depression. They rented a home ever after that. Bessie could no longer teach, as married, female teachers were not hired in those days.

Emma, their first born, came along in due time, then Laura. The twins, Charles and Carl, were quite a surprise to the family, and James, the last of the children. Dr. Brayfield attended each of the births.

After the children were grown, Bessie needed to supplement the family income and became the "baby nurse" at the local hospital.

Her husband Charlie died in 1956. For 29 years Bessie lived as a widow until her death in June 1985. She was buried alongside Charlie near her parents, at Knob Prairie Baptist Cemetery. She was 94 years old at the time of her death.

Mom did the best she could; she knew what was best for us. That's what leads to our longevity. Mom worked in the hospital at night, walked all of the way out there, through rain, snow, or anything. She was a hard worker and it didn't hurt her a bit. She lived a good long life.

I remember my mother having a giving heart. If we needed something even though she didn't have the money to buy it, somehow she would find a way to get it for us if it were essential. Later in life when we were all on our own and making it in the world, she gave of her meager means to child care charities around the world. She never learned to spend what she had to indulge on herself.

Charlie Lutes by Emma

Charlie (Charles W.) Lutes was born the eighth child of Cyrus and Louisa Hunter Lutes, (ed. note: the West Virginia birth registry lists his birthday in May 1867, but Charlie always celebrated his birthday in April), the eighth of fifteen children. They lived on his father, David's farm on Taylor's Ridge near Moundsville, West Virginia. In his will, David gave the farm to Cyrus.

Charlie was not fond of farming, but when he married Belle Bennett in June 1894, they lived on a dairy farm in the Franklin District in Marshall County, West Virginia. Later he worked as a laborer for the railroad in Moundsville. They had one son, William C. Lutes. Charlie and Belle divorced in 1905. Not much else is known about this marriage or about Charlie's life until he came to Christopher in about 1918-19.

John, Charlie's brother, was a contractor hired to finish building the Methodist Church in Christopher. Charlie came to Christopher to work for John. When the work was completed, John moved to California. In Christopher, Charlie had met Bessie Duckworth. They courted and were married in March 1920. John's wife, Levina, was Bessie's maid of honor.

Charlie and Bessie raised five children; Emma, named for her grandmother; Laura, named after Charlie's sister; the twins, Charles and Carl, each named with parts of Charlie's full name; and Jim.

During his life in Christopher, Charlie was in City government for a number of years. He was Chief of Police, Street Commissioner, and Fire Chief. During the Great Depression he held various jobs, including Justice of the Peace.

Charlie belonged to the Christopher Methodist Church and used his beautiful bass voice in the church choir. Also, he always had a nice garden as a result of his upbringing on the farm in West Virginia.

Charlie lost a leg to blood poisoning and was in the hospital for a short time. He hated his stay there, as it was his first time as a patient. All older persons that he had known went to the hospital to die. He was not a very cooperative patient and begged to go home.

Charlie died at home on November 2, 1956. He was 89 years old. Charlie and Bessie were buried beside Bessie's parents in Knob Prairie Cemetery in Franklin County, Illinois.

Editor's note: This editor was told years later that he was in Charlie and Bessie's home when Charlie died. Being only four years old at the time, not much was remembered of the event until told of this fact and recalling memories of seeing his grandmother Bessie giving Charlie a sponge bath as he lay in bed in the bedroom at the end of a long hallway. Charlie seemed very fussy with Bessie during the bath. Another memory was of the door to Charlie's bedroom being closed and the young child wondering why he was not allowed to see his grandfather.

Charlie Lutes by Carl and Charles "Peanut" Lutes

They had a man out in the woods. They were going to hang him. And then dad, the town constable at the time, went out there and he said to them, "Let this man go and if you don't I'm going to shoot you." Somebody made a movement toward dad's gun and he shot the man's ear off. Later, a man said to us, "I was so proud of your dad."

No one ever told us this except that man. The only proof is that man's statement. We don't remember his name except he was related to the Allard's. He had lived in Christopher. He was young and he saw this. He said, "I was so proud of your dad." But, mom would never let a gun in the house.

Dad came to Christopher to be with his brother John and to work. He worked into his seventies. He did every kind of a job you can imagine. He did manual labor, but usually he was the boss. He was like that -- he'd take any kind of job, like police magistrate, fire chief, road commissioner, and manual labor, too.

When he was working a union job, scabs came in and tried to break it up. Dad got into a fight and got hit over the head with a beer bottle. He came home all bloodied up.

But, he was well known around town and was kind of a big shot for a while, political, a Democrat. He

*Carl, Emma, Bessie &
Charlie Lutes, mid to late-1930s*

moved from one job to another. He never had one real job, like a profession. They were redoing the city reservoir in Christopher and they put dad in charge of it. He took us kids out there with him to see the work. We watched; it was very interesting. He was over all the guys that worked with the shovels and moved the stones. One guy was a timekeeper, that's all he did. He was sick and couldn't do hard labor.

We were so proud of our dad because he was a big shot boss of all this. To us it was a big project. He'd get jobs like that, mostly through political connections.

Charlie and Bessie Lutes by Emma, Carl and Charles "Peanut" Lutes

Charlie and Bessie met at church. Charlie was still living with his brother John Lutes at the time he met Bessie. John was a carpenter. John came here because it was a mining town and they were building a lot of buildings. He built the Methodist Church among others. He was in charge of it as a contractor. We met Levina Lutes, John Lutes' wife, and their children, Russell and the girl they adopted. They were all very bright and industrious. Russell later became a photographer. He liked dad so much.

Charlie and Bessie were opposites -- she read and read, often climbing up a tree, as she later related to us, to be alone in her world of solitude and books. She read everything she could get her hands on -- including Dickens -- and, sometimes between harvest and turning up the soil in the spring while still living on her parent's farm she managed to take classes at a regional teacher's college preparing to be a teacher, often riding a trusty horse through autumn rain and winter snow to get there.

Charlie, on the other hand, loved conversation and being with people, which was probably another reason he was always running for one elected office or another, including sheriff, street commissioner, fire chief, and police magistrate. Along with his dog, he made a walk to town to see his buddies practically every day until just before he died. His nephew Russell once confided, although he loved attention he wasn't enamored with responsibility.

Dad was very well liked. Everyone in town knew him. Socially he was very impressive. Mom must have been "knocked over" by him when they met. Here's this guy from the east, good looking and very friendly and affectionate. She never knew anyone like that except from books. She was the opposite of dad. She was hardworking, responsible, and all business. But, opposites often connect.

Mom often gave this example of dad's impracticality. She sent him to the store for some bananas. He came home with a whole stalk! We couldn't finish all of them all before they'd go bad. Mom asked him why he bought so many and dad said he got them at a good price. It didn't occur to him that we'd get sick of them and the bananas couldn't hold up until we could finish them all. He got them at a good price. He thought she would be so happy and meet him at the door with open arms.

When we were kids, she would allow him to drink beer. We had an old ice box and dad put a couple of beers in there. We had gotten into them, drank one, refilled it with water, and recapped it. Dad came home all thirsty and hot and went to the ice box for one. After he had one sip he threw that bottle down and knew immediately that his children had been into his beer and came after us. Mom said, "You'll not have any more beer in the house because of the kids."

Charlie spent hours with his children in the evenings. He was outgoing, affectionate, and generally mild-mannered. Charlie identified with children and shared their ability to capture the joy of the moment, oblivious to the consequences. For him, every day was a payday and every day was a play day, neither of which lasted long enough.

He drank too much later in life. It came on slowly. He really wasn't a drunk, it's just that one beer set him off. He'd get high on one beer. Lots of people could have six or seven. One is all dad needed. Then he'd get religion and talk a lot.

Bessie, who had been teaching for several years before she met Charlie, had to give up her job when she married. It was custom then. In addition to raising five children, Bessie cleaned houses for other people to supplement the family income. She cut their grass, removed the ashes from their furnaces, and shoveled their show. She wanted her children to have what they needed.

When Bessie's mother died, she left each of her children $100 dollars. Bessie invested hers in a washing machine, a rarity at the time if not a luxury. For the next fifteen years she took in washings. During this time she prepared herself to become a nurse, her specialty was caring for newborn babies. She worked as a nurse in the town's hospital until she retired, devoting to hundreds of newborn babies the same care she had tendered to her five children.

Charlie had more of an aptitude for music and fun and Bessie for literary pursuits and hard work. Early memories of them include Charlie signing "Rock-a-bye Baby" and "Little Dickie Bird" as he held his children in his lap. He was blessed with a fine, deep voice and loved to sing in the church choir, often holding the notes a split second longer than the others to ensure he was heard.

And Bessie, she would read stories like "The Ant and the Grasshopper" and "The Little Train that Wouldn't Give Up" from a book of stories for children while guiding her children's fingers over each word she read. She joined a book club later in life that sent her various books, usually a novel or biography. She continued as a teacher into her eighties for her Sunday school class of middle-aged to elderly women, all of whom she outlived, as she lived to age 94.

Their marriage wasn't perfect as there were disagreements from time to time, some may say even clashes. She was a strong wife and he often a stubborn husband. Opposites do attract, as the old adage surely holds true in the case of Charlie and Bessie. She may have been a character out of a novel by Hawthorne and he out of Dickens -- her industrialism versus his fantasies or her sense of responsibility versus his playfulness.

Regardless, they made their marriage work, raised five successful children, and are now buried beside each other in a small cemetery not too far from her parent's old farm.

The Great Depression by Others

A scholar said in 2008 or 2009 that "this recession was as dire as the Great Depression." If he just knew what the Great Depression was really like, he'd be ashamed to even compare 2008 with the Great Depression of the 1930s. People lined up to get food. The CCC was a wonderful program by President Roosevelt. All the youth who had nowhere to go nor knew what to do came to work under the CCC program to improve the country. They made the lodge at Giant City. The CCC was like the army. You had to dress a certain way, get up, and work.

Grandma Lutes' Scrapbook by her Grandson

Grandma Lutes kept a scrapbook of items she found interesting, such as clippings from newspapers, and old church bulletins. Most of them were from the 1950-60s, long after her children had left home. It was interesting that there were no clippings of her family and few, if any of her friends and neighbors in her scrapbook.

Most of her newspaper clippings were about women and what they had accomplished in a day when women were expected to stay at home and raise their children. An example of a woman with a successful career in grandma's scrapbook was Marion Mayer, the Vice-President and Executive Editor of *American Home* magazine. Another was Marlys Watters, a talented concert singer. Finally, there was Dorothy Block and Rosa Dietcher who were owners of Doll's Outfitters.

There were as many as forty-six clippings of women and their accomplishments -- some famous women such as Golda Meir, Ann Landers, Marion Anderson, Sally Rand, Eleanor Roosevelt, and Helen Keller -- and other women whose names are now lost to history.

It was interesting that many the clippings named the women by their husband's name; that is Mrs. Jerome F. Duggan and Mrs. Larson Carey, never to mention the woman's given first name. Also noted was Clare Williams, the "top lady in Republican national political circles," was mentioned as the "Assistant G.O.P. national chairman (ed. note: not chairwoman) in charge of woman's activities." Times were different in her day.

It was amusing to see citations like Mrs. Jerome F. Duggan listed as a "colonel" on the staff of Governor Frank G. Clement of Tennessee and Perle Mesta, ambassador to Luxembourg, who was said to be known for her sometimes outlandish and always lavish parties.

Equally marvelous were clippings of women pioneers like Joanne Alford who had a Bachelor of Science degree in air transportation engineering and a pilot's license and held a job as a materials and process engineer with the Martin Company in Baltimore, or Dr. Jessie L. Ternberg, the first resident in surgery at Barnes Hospital in St. Louis. And Kay Williams who was a partner with her husband in the Law Firm that bared her name. These occupations and professions were closed to women for so many years.

It was awesome to feel the enthusiasm in the clippings of Grandma Moses, ninety-eight year old artistic painter at that time. Then there was a story about Sarah Josepha Hale, considered the mother of our modern Thanksgiving Day celebration when she convinced President Abraham Lincoln in 1863 to make the fourth Thursday in November a national day of giving thanks. She also authored "Mary Had a Little Lamb" that is popular among so many children's books and poems. No less notable was Stella Bennett who retired from teaching at age eighty, the oldest active teacher at that time.

There were very few clippings of men in her scrapbook, but an interesting one was of 106 year old Sylvester Melvin who was still farming and was the elected secretary of the Greene County Mutual Fire Insurance Company, a position to which he was elected fifty-eight consecutive years. He was born about 1842, remembered the Civil War, President Lincoln, and General Grant. He had graduated from Illinois Wesleyan College in the 1870s or so.

More traditional scrapbook items in Grandma's book were articles on religion and copies of prayers. There were many lovely pictures, thoughtful writings, poetry, and clippings on nurses and teachers, of which she had been one. Articles about residents and former residents of Christopher were also kept.

Personal mementoes were few, such as old photographs and a copy of the Christopher Progress dedicated to the history of Christopher. However, these may have been added later by her children.

Her more interesting mementoes were of her church membership cards, being so devoted to the Methodist Church and devoutly religious.

Finally there was a receipt from Local Union #13385 of the U.M.W. of A. for dues paid of $1.50 on December 15, 1948. I wish I knew why she kept this. Was it shuffled into her scrapbook by mistake? Or was there some other special reason for keeping it?

I wish I could have known her reason for keeping these things, or that a revelation from on high would give me insight into her mind at the time. These items were important to her. They are the last of the few remaining tangible items she touched and that we have left with which to appreciate, smile, and celebrate.

Fortunately, however, the most important part of her that we have is her blood that runs through our veins every day -- and the reason we are all here to celebrate her and all of our ancestors.

An Item from Grandma Lutes' Scrapbook

Unknown News Article --

I hope all women who were notified, due to a clerical mix up, that they had been selected Kansas *Mother of the Year* weren't too disappointed at the mistake. They shouldn't have been. For no committee can really know which one of all the wonderful mothers anywhere deserve to be elevated above the rest.

Only a woman's own children really know what kind of a mother she is. So, the most honors that can come to any mother, isn't a committee's nod.

The highest honor that any mother can ever hope for comes from her own children. If they admire as well as love her, if they find as the years go by that her teachings are a part of their character, if they are proud of her, if they find companionship with her, if there is no doubt in their minds but that they have the finest mother in the world -- then that mother is truly honored.

What the rest of the world thinks or says about a mother isn't really important. It's how her children feel about her that counts. There is no reliable standard by which a mother can be judged by outsiders.

The fact that a woman's children are successful may or may not mean that she has been a better mother than one whose children have not climbed so high. The fact that a woman has made her own mark in the world doesn't necessarily mean that she has been a better mother than one whose only contribution to the world is to have made a happy home.

So it is only in the hearts of her children that a mother is honestly judged. If they think she is the most wonderful mother in the world then she is. No committee can hand her that honor or take it away.

Emma and Laura Lutes by Carl and Charles "Peanut" Lutes

Laura was a lot like her dad, very sociable. Fortunately for Laura, she married Bus. That was a wonderful thing for her. He disciplined her. We never thought she'd put up with it, but she loved that man like you'd never know.

She was like a wild child in every way. She was the first one to learn how to ice skate. She used to go to the roller rink, that's where she met Bus. In those days, roller rinks were very popular. She was a very good skater, rhythmic and athletic.

She was a very good dancer, too. She wasn't supposed to dance. It was a sin. But, she did anyway. That gives you a clue of her wild side.

She dropped out of high school, but mom wasn't going to put up with that. She made Laura work around the house, so Laura went back to school. She went back to school fast once she had to do all that work at home.

She was very beautiful, a real blond with black eyes. She had lots of boyfriends hanging around. I'll never forget once when she and Emma were going somewhere. They were both dating guys from Valier then. In those days, boys were bashful. So the boys would whistle when they arrived and the girls would run outside to meet them. Once they whistled and dad went out and said, "Get the hell out of here, we got no dogs here!" So they couldn't go out that night with these boys.

Emma didn't have too many boyfriends. Todd Taylor was a boyfriend for four or five years. He lived in Valier. Todd was going to be a preacher. He was, you might say, passive. He had no plans. I guess Emma decided she didn't like that.

One night Todd and Emma with Bus and Laura were going to go fishing at the Big Muddy or somewhere. Mom said, "You're not going unless you take the three boys with you" (ed. note: Emma and Laura's three younger brothers.) What kind of a date is that? They made a campfire and had marshmallows. Can you imagine a date with your little brothers along? Most parents were very careful about their kids. They watched them carefully.

Charles "Peanut" Lutes by Emma Smith and Carl Lutes

Charles Lutes, son of Charlie and Bessie Duckworth Lutes, was born in September 1926 in Christopher, IL. He was born two minutes prior to his fraternal twin Carl. He was a commercial truck driver for many years, driving for two different trucking companies.

With his father's background in community service, Charles began his involvement at an early age in the Christopher Police and Fire Departments. It was reported that he would "hang around" the Fire and Police Departments when he was an adolescent, pretending to be a "Junior Policeman." Many of the police officers and firefighters called him "pee wee" because of his diminutive size as a child. Among other nicknames he picked up during his childhood was "Peanuts." No one knows why he was tagged with this nickname, but there are many suspicions.

Charles became more involved in the Fire Department in about 1960. He joined the Fire Department as an official volunteer in about 1963 under former Fire Chief Pep Trogolo and continued volunteering into the 1980s under Chief Raymond Bione.

Charles was appointed Fire Chief in 1986 by Christopher Mayor Gary Bartolotti. He has served in that capacity for about 30 years. His fellow firefighters say that Chief Lutes is strict, but does not hold a grudge when someone makes a mistake.

It is often said that Charles learned all he knows about firefighting by having extinguished thousands of fires over the years and learning from each one. "No two fires are the same," he is quoted as saying. Learning while on the job, supplemented by many hours of state-sponsored training in Springfield, shaped his knowledge of firefighting.

Christopher has a limited budget for their Fire Department. Chief Lutes decided to help raise money for his Department by standing in street intersections with his men and collecting donations in small buckets. Determined to buy the best and safest firefighting equipment for his men, Charles has raised thousands of dollars over the years.

Charles was described by his peers as "all business while working, but liked to play when he was not working."

An example of his business side, firefighters tell a story about the time that Charles fell off the fire truck and received a rather deep cut on his head. He refused medical attention until after the fire was extinguished. Afterwards his head required several stitches.

Examples of their playful sides include an incident when his fellow firefighters painted his fingernails as a prank while he was "napping" in the fire department's office. Since sleeping was his favorite activity in between fire calls, Charles would occasionally awake to find strips of paper taped over his eyes.

The job of a firefighter is a hazardous one. Not only is fighting fires dangerous, but also apparently are the comments made by his fellow firefighters to his wife, Loretta.

For example, when Loretta asked one of the firefighters where she could find Charles, the firefighter told her that he was at the local bar. She was not amused, not realizing that the firefighter was just joking with her.

Another time, during a city parade and day of celebration, Loretta asked a firefighter if she could ride in the parade car with Charles, who was serving as the parade's grandmaster. Apparently, the firefighter told Loretta that she was not allowed in the parade because Charles had told him "a woman's place is in the home, not in public." It is not certain how many stitches Charles needed after he "reportedly" had made that comment.

Charles continues to stay involved with the firefighters in and around the Christopher area. He no longer participates in the physical activity connected with fighting a fire due to being challenged by his age. He serves mostly in a consulting position. However, his immense knowledge of fires is an invaluable resource that is admired by the other firefighters.

Thank you Charles "Pee Wee, Peanuts" Lutes for your continued service to your community and personal involvement in the lives of so many.

The Distinguished Career of Carl Lutes from Various Sources

Carl W. Lutes, son of Charlie and Bessie Duckworth Lutes, was born in September 1926 in Christopher two minutes after his fraternal twin Charles. He spent most of his life in the arts, pursuing careers in both English and music -- as a high school teacher in his hometown of Christopher, as a member of the SIU English Department for five years, and a middle school and high school teacher in New York City.

He has also been principal flutist with the St. Louis Symphony Orchestra and the Longines Symphonette, a national radio orchestra, and concertized throughout the U.S., Canada, and Mexico. He was the personal flutist with Metropolitan opera star Roberta Peters for one year. In 1962, he made an interesting tour of the Soviet Union in an orchestra sponsored by the State Department, unexpectedly finding himself in Moscow during the Cuban missile crisis.

Carl enrolled at SIU, then Southern Illinois Normal University, before graduating from high school. World War II was raging and all males were expected to do military service; so after a year at SIU, he left for the Navy, playing in the Navy band in Washington, D.C., before assignment to the battleship, USS Washington. After the war, he returned to SIU to finish his bachelor's degree, then off to Columbia University for a master's degree in music and further graduate study at the Paris Conservatory and the Sorbonne, where he received degrees in Flute and French Language and Culture.

In 1957 at the "Music under the Stars Festival" at McAndrew Stadium, Lutes was featured as Honored Southern Illinois Musician. Carl is a two-degree SIU graduate with a Bachelor's degree in 1948 and a Master's degree in 1959. He taught English at SIU Carbondale. He moved to New York City where he taught English. He retired to Somers, NY and later moved back to Carbondale, IL.

During his studies at SIU, Carl was granted a university scholarship. In gratitude, he has established endowed scholarships for a deserving student from his hometown and for exceptional students in the fields of music and English.

In April 2015, Carl received the 2015 SIU Distinguished Alumni Award for Cultural Impact. In the spring 2016, Carl promised a major bequest to the University Museum of his art and furniture collection. Moreover, he provided funds to assure the care of this outstanding collection. From January 22 to March 6, 2016, Carl had his longstanding love and collection of textiles exhibited at the SIU Museum. The collection featured some of his Persian miniatures, rugs and tapestries. (Persian pictorial rug, Kashan region, circa 1880)

In October 2018, a new gallery was opened at the SIU Museum, featuring his personal and unique collection pieces from the Renaissance era. Included in the gallery were Flemish and French tapestries, Hercules and the Nemean Lion sculpture, Italian walnut dante and sgabello chairs, and paintings depicting St. Michael the Archangel subduing Lucifer, among others. "Historically the Renaissance was a period of creative innovation and cultural magnificence," said John Pollitz, dean of Library Affairs. "We are fortunate to have such a unique opportunity to highlight art, furniture and tapestries from this period, thanks to Mr. Lutes."

Lutes love for art first started at SIU as a young student enrolled in a foundational art appreciation class. After developing as an artist and spending years collecting each unique piece, it only made sense for the collection to come full circle back to SIU. For Lutes, his purpose is quite simple. "My purpose mainly for leaving it here is for students to learn,"

Lutes said. Students who are taking similar art classes can examine the work and learn from it for their own study, Lutes explained.

Jim Lutes -- "A Brother Remembers" by Carl Lutes

I remember very well the day Jim Lutes was born in July 1930 -- although my brother Charles and I were not yet four years old. In Christopher, as in most towns in those days, babies were usually born in the home; so to remove the Lutes children from underfoot and to spare them the specifics of the mysterious ordeal, we were dispatched to neighbors for safe keeping.

At that time you didn't pay for baby sitters. Baby sitting was a neighborly expectation, although it had to be a real emergency for parents to leave their children with someone outside the family circle. In most large families the older children were expected to look after their younger siblings -- which proves that Jim's birth was a special occasion in the Lutes household.

Emma and Laura, then nine and eight, were whisked off to the Schultzes or the Oldanis, and Charles and I were left with Andrew Kauzlarich, who lived across the street. There we sat on the front porch swing and watched as the doctor arrived at our house on Cherry Street and several neighbor women came and went. Later, when we saw the scrawny thing everybody was fussing about, we couldn't understand why there had been so much hubbub.

Jim was always a scrawny kid, pale, almost frail; like an insignificant seed just waiting to sprout, one day without warning he suddenly sprang up tall, broad-chested, strong, and well-proportioned. Everybody seemed surprised except Jim, who was, nevertheless, happy with the transformation. Although he was not overly confident in school or in certain social situations, he had the utmost confidence in his physical skills -- which served him well as an athlete and soldier, and in his profession later on.

As baby Jim got bigger and bigger, Charles and I were expected to watch over him more and more, which was all right until we got to an age when we wanted to hang out with the gang. Jim admired his older brothers so much he followed them everywhere they went -- except that his brothers, as they got older, became less enchanted with the idea of Little Brother always tagging along.

But that didn't stop Jim. He'd wait until we were on our way hiking, or fishing, or wherever boys go at that age. Then suddenly he appeared out of nowhere, too far from home to be sent back alone. Younger brother or not, he always planned well. On one occasion he turned up just as were climbing into the back of a truck we'd hitched a ride with, heading to Benton Lake for the afternoon. At that point, there was no choice; we had to take him along.

Jim, the grateful brother, as an act of thanks for letting him come along, or maybe as an act of contrition, rewarded us with an unexpected plunge from a ten-foot diving board. We couldn't understand where he had learned to dive like that: he was hardly seven, and besides, most of our swimming had been in local cow ponds or shallow creeks. Looking back, it's easy to understand now. Jim was a natural athlete.

Which is what kept him interested in school, although my mother wrote that, after Charles and I left for the Navy, Jim played hooky on and off for at least a year, seeking older friends as surrogate brothers, staying out late, swigging beer with his cronies, trying to grow up. It may have helped: by the time he entered high school, he'd settled down some. Four years of playing on the varsity football team also helped.

Jim was fast. On the track team his specialty was the 100-yard or the 50-yard dash. He also made up one-quarter of the rely team. A sprinter by nature, he made an excellent quarterback for the football team. He was agile and unafraid. The toughest line of heavies didn't intimidate him. He'd charge right through them -- or make a decent try.

He was a good boxer, too, fast and plucky. Under his senior picture in the *Christopherian* is a caption: "LOVES TO BOX!" Also under the picture is a summation of his athletic accomplishments: Football 1-4; Track 1-4; C-Club 1-4; Boxing 2-4.

A pugilist he was -- but a gentle one, modest too, and affectionate, even sentimental. He had lots of friends: Bob Rude as a child, Johnny

Moore, Vic Kretz, and Elmer Covalesky in high school, to name a few special ones.

Along with Jim's gentleness came a natural respect for others. During his last two years of high school, I was a teacher at Christopher High School. Surprisingly, he always addressed me as Mr. Lutes when with the other students. No one asked him to do it, or had to explain to him why he should.

He was just as respectful of his sisters and parents -- and protective of them as well. His father was sixty-one years old when Jim was born and already developing vision problems that weren't helped by an occasional evening bash at Pete's tavern. Even as a child, Jim worried about his father, especially when he didn't come home on time; then he would go out to look for him to "lead him home," as he phrased it. He knew just where to look too.

Despite his soft streak, however, Jim was no angel. He had a temper. If someone crossed him up or betrayed him, he'd come back with both fists-- and hard -- although that didn't happen very often. His natural vocabulary was a physical one, which was especially noticeable when he climbed behind the wheel of a car. You'd think he was riding a bronco. More than once he got grounded for bronco-ing my Pontiac convertible.

Jim graduated from high school in 1950, and, although he didn't make valedictorian, we were glad enough just to know he'd made it. So was he, especially since the Korean War was raging, and Jim was sure to be drawn into it.

Within months of graduation Jim found himself in the U.S. Air Force, stationed in Hawaii, the last Lutes to leave the nest. Later, he told me that on the night he left for service he realized after he'd started for the train that he'd forgotten some important papers at home. When he came back to retrieve them, he found both his mother and father still sitting there crying.

Jim was good to his parents. Every month he sent half of his pay home, although military pay in those days was meager, even for an airplane mechanic who could repair heavy bombers sent back to Hawaii from the Korean Theater. Restoring such a marvelous piece of machinery to its original beauty gave Jim great pleasure. It was also good training for a future profession.

Not long after Jim came back from military service, he met and fell in love with Lillian Beasley of Du Quoin. They were married in October 1955 and moved into a quaint little house in Old Du Quoin (ed. note: Jim and Lillian were married in Flora, Illinois by Walter Smith.) It was small, homey, in good shape, in a country setting with lots of trees around and plenty of fresh air, a real love nest. That's where they lived when their first child Nancy arrived.

When Jim first came back from the Air Force, jobs were not easy to find, but he managed to get work at the Chevrolet garage in Christopher, doing mechanical and body work. Later he took a position with Chevrolet in Carbondale and performed so well he was asked to teach in a vocational and technical division of Rend Lake College.

"I won't put up with students fooling around in class!" I didn't say a word, but there had to be a smile encroaching somewhere on my face.

A second child, Steven Robert, was born four years after Nancy. Their parents gave both children good care and lots of attention, and Jim worked hard in his job to give them the many things he never had, including a spacious old house updated into a beautiful and comfortable home. Jim was then working for Freeman Coal Mine as a wheel operator, a huge machine that stripped the land of coal then restored it afterwards according to federal environmental standards. He liked the job and did well financially, often working overtime several times a week until he retired.

Jim liked to travel, and so did I. He had dreamed of going everywhere after retirement, so the two of us flew to Hawaii for two weeks as a starter. It was the first time he'd been back since the war. He had lots of stories to tell as he showed me around the islands.

Next we took a cruise on the Royal Caribbean Line to Southeast Asia for another two weeks. It was a beautiful ship, making calls at Singapore, Java, Bali, Malaysia, and several exotic islands. Being together again after forty-five years was like old times. We reminisced all day about Christopher and the crazy things we used to do.

The Lutes Family
By Emma & Others

One evening when I wanted to be alone for awhile, accustomed to solitude, I mentioned that I was going topside for a breath of fresh air. Within five minutes who should suddenly emerge from behind a bulkhead? Yes, little brother Jim. It was indeed old times again.

On the flight back to St. Louis, we made plans for other trips. Jim wanted to see the whole world. I was for that!

But it wasn't to be. In less than a year, the body that had served Jim so well was beginning to fail him. Whether suffering from the jolt of having lived too hard, or just tired and overworked, or simply part of a Great Plan which neither iron will nor the strongest body can override, Jim died of heart failure in October 1997 at the age of sixty-seven, much too early, we thought, leaving behind a family he loved so much.

The Great Plan was not so great, I thought at the time. But maybe it was. It granted a wife and two children he dearly loved, four grandchildren he literally worshipped -- and who knows how many great grandchildren yet to come? Also, his two sisters and two brothers still miss him, as well as eight nieces and nephews.

As Jim once confessed to me, "What matters above everything else to me is family. It's everything!"

Yes, it is, and if my little brother could only come back again, I'd let him tag along everywhere I went.

The Duckworth Family by Emma

Granddad, William Duckworth and Emma Alston, were married about sixteen years before Bessie was born in 1889. Granddad grew his own tobacco on their farm and smoked a pipe continuously. His philosophy was, "one is supposed to have a hard time in life." Granddad died in his fifties from kidney failure or prostate issues in 1905. Grandma continued to live on the farm until about 1930.

Duckworth Reunion, 1939

Granddad was taken to the cemetery for burial by horse and wagon. It was common practice at that time for neighbors to help with the funeral arrangements; washing and dressing the bodies of the deceased, making the casket, packing the casket with ice in the summer when it was hot, and digging and burying the casket after the graveside service.

Their first born, Charles E. Duckworth, lived to age 33 when he died of pneumatic fever. He was buried at Osage Cemetery near Colp, Illinois along side of his unnamed sister who died as an infant. Orrie E. Duckworth died in a boating accident near Fort Smith, Arkansas after she married Bob Smith (ed. note: Orrie's cemetery marker was actually found in Manila, Arkansas, not Fort Smith). They had a fishing business. Lamont Duckworth, a brother, died at age 34 (ed. note: per findagrave.com). Only their children Raleigh, Bessie, Ralph and Cora Duckworth lived to old age, the latter three into their nineties.

Grandma made all of the family's clothes, except their coats and overalls. When the children went to school, the daughters had two dresses to wear, plus a sun dress. For the next school year, one of the dresses was worn while doing chores and a new dress was made for school. The girls wore slips and underwear made of flannel, tight at the waist, going down to the knee, and buttoned. High top shoes and overshoes were worn to school about one and a half miles away, which they walked. They took an open lunch bucket filled with a sandwich of whatever was available and leftover pie. The school was heated with wood furnaces, later with coal. Wood stoves and furnaces were used at home, as well.

Food, such as fruit, was put on straw and covered with more straw and dirt to help it keep longer in the fall. There was a root cellar that kept food from freezing in the winter.

Their toys were china dolls, a cradle made of walnut, jump rope, group games, climbing trees, and reading books whenever they could get one. They visited neighbors a lot during lunch and sometimes overnight. Bessie learned to use a thimble and thread to sew, piecing quilt squares together and sewing around the edges of table cloths by the time she was six. Later she learned to use her mother's foot-propelled sewing machine. At age twelve, she took an old coat and repaired it for her neighbor who was poor.

Bessie's brother Raleigh Duckworth was a large man, in fact all of the Duckworth's that we knew, except grandma, had large bones. Raleigh was dark headed and we remember him with black, curly hair. Raleigh and his son Herschel worked the Duckworth farm until it was sold to Bob Buntin. We always enjoyed having the Duckworth families come to our home to spend the day because we enjoyed playing with our cousins.

Cousins Chalen, Fred, Loreta, and Billy came to visit us and were the ones that we knew best. Billy went off to Chicago. He was always a lot of fun to be around so we missed him.

Uncle Ralph lived north of Sesser for a while with his two daughters. We used to go visit. We would take a train we called the "Dinky" to Sesser and then walk from town to their farm. We may have spent a week with them. We got to know our two cousins, Dorothy and Vivian, pretty well. They had a boy who died. Later, Dorothy had a son, Jack, and Uncle Ralph and his wife, Floy raised him.

Aunt Floy was a good cook. One time they had a harvest and made banana pudding in a tub for the harvest hands. The air was full of chaff that came off the wheat. In those days there were a lot of flies and before they could eat the harvest dinner, all of the ladies took towels and from the back of the house to the front and shooed flies out before the guys could come in to eat dinner. It was a different world because we grew up in town without all of the animals and there were no screens back then. Ralph farmed and worked in the mines.

About four o'clock every afternoon we would get all the cows to come home so they could be milked. Even milking cows was strange to me. I remember Aunt Floy put the milk in a churn and made butter and buttermilk. We learned a lot on the farm.

Mom taught school in Christopher when her nieces, Raleigh's daughters Mable and Myrtle Duckworth, came to live with her to finish their high school education. Myrtle even went to SINU in Carbondale for one year before she was married.

Aunt Cora did not married until she was thirty-five or so. Her husband worked in Missouri south of St. Louis somewhere. She was a tall woman with big bones with light brown hair. She was all business.

Editor's note: Carl Lutes related the story of the time when his dad traded a crank-style Victor-Victoria phonograph to Bessie's nephew Herschel for a hog. Charlie and Bessie butchered the hog and lived on it to get through the winter months that year. Herschel wanted the phonograph for his wife Arvada who loved to listen to music and dance to it. Another story was related to the regular Duckworth reunions that were usually held on Duckworth's farm. Charlie and Bessie paid a man who had a truck to take them to the farm, which was out in the country. Rains had saturated the area for days leading up to the reunion. Since the only way to get to the farm was on unpaved country lanes, the truck got stuck in one particularly muddy area. The man nearly burned up his truck motor trying to get the truck out of the muck, but was unsuccessful in doing so. Later that day another man and his team of horses pulled the truck out of the mess. Having been stuck for the better part of the day, the family headed back to Christopher rather than proceed on to the reunion.

Emma Alston Duckworth by Carl and Charles "Peanut" Lutes

Dad went to Uncle Ralph's one time to see them and grandma. There was no heat in their house. It was cold. He brought grandma to our home. That's why she lived with us. She'd leave to visit her other children for a while from time to time, then come back to live with us. Dad was very good to her.

She had her own room. She smoked a pipe and dad would say, "I like to see an old lady smoke a pipe." She had all of her old fashion furniture and her "famous" wooden trunk. Grandma Duckworth had a bottle of whiskey in her wooden trunk when she lived with us. That was her medicine.

She would tell weird, gruesome stories. One time she saw that we were mistreating our little brother. I can still see her sticking up her little fists at us from her rocking chair. She told us a story about these two boys who were mean and didn't like their little brother. One day the two boys cut their little brother to pieces. When the parents came home they found him in pieces and spanked the two boys. She had a lot of stories like that, and many about animals and lions.

She stayed with us till she died. She died in our house. Mom had to bathe her and take care of her before she died. Her coffin was placed in our house in her room. It was there for a few days. When we had the funeral, all the neighbors came and brought food.

Editor's note: The following was written mostly by Emma about Walter's early years. She wrote this account of his early life after Walter died in 1998.

Walter Smith's Childhood by Emma

Walter A. Smith was born in August 1915 in Union County, Illinois to Ross and Emma Smith. The little farm where he was born near Alto Pass, in the shadow of Bald Knob hill, belonged to Nathaniel and Mary Pirtle, his maternal grandparents. The farm was on a creek. The farm house was a two room house with a wood burning stove in the middle of the room. It had no running water. The

Hubert (sitting), Artie & Walter, 1920s

closest source of water was a spring just down the road a piece. It had to be heated on the wood burning stove.

When he was two years old, there was a flood and the family decided to cross the creek and when both parents needed to paddle, Walter fell overboard. They quickly got him back onboard and got to their destination.

In 1918 when there was a flu epidemic, Walter succumbed and almost died.

When Ross and Emma decided they couldn't make a living on this small farm, they moved to Murphysboro. Walter received most of his grade schooling there.

The 1925 Great Tornado sped through Murphysboro. Walter was in fifth grade. His dad worked at the electric company stoking the furnace. His dad quickly climbed into the large furnace, which was not in use, and it probably saved his life. However, he breathed in so much soot from the furnace that he had black lung disease the rest of his life. Walter's mother, Emma, went to his school as soon as the storm abated. She found Artie, who informed her that Walter had returned to his schoolroom to retrieve his cap.

In one of his sermons, Walter spoke of spending two or three weeks each summer on his grandparent's farm, learning rural ways and traditions. He mostly remembered the animals, his grandmother's cooking, and the hard life on the farm. There was no air-conditioning or refrigerators, and a light bulb was strung on an electrical line hanging from the ceiling. There was no ice to keep things cool. In fact the milk was kept in the cistern which was the coolest place to keep things. But these times were memories of family-life and meals together that he treasured throughout his lifetime.

He related one story about a time when his grandmother was out of sugar and sent him to the country store to trade eggs gathered on the farm for sugar. They called the country store a "slap out," coming from the expression that the store was always "slap out of this or that, or something else." His grandmother wrapped two-dozen eggs in a towel and put them in a basket and Walter started out on three-miles of dusty roads to the nearest "slap-out" to trade the eggs for sugar. The "slap-out's" kindly store owner took the eggs and gave young Walter sugar for him to take back home.

This story ends with supper, one of the greatest meals of his life. There was his grandmother's usual plates of meat, potatoes and gravy, hot biscuits, and cobbler or pie. He remembered the biscuits as "light as a feather and piping hot," and as a friend describe them, "the first bite was a half moon and second a total eclipse." Finally, there was the big, juicy blackberry cobbler to top off the meal.

Walter credited the best of modern American-life to these small farms and simpler times that shaped their independence, self reliance, and resourcefulness. Twelve children grew up on his grandmother's farm and many of her grandchildren shared their summers there.

Walter's parents joined the Centenary Methodist Church after a revival that they attended and his dad felt a "call to the ministry." Walter's father got a little religious schooling and was sent to his first charge.

Walter's Childhood
By Emma

One time his dad took him to the home of the Sunday school superintendent who was dying of cancer. The people outside of the man's room said that he wouldn't know them. As a matter of fact, when they walked into the room he was in a coma.

But his dad spoke to him, "Brother Johnson." And he responded, immediately wide awake. And his dad said, "How is everything?" He said, "I've seen the other side and it's all right." Walter had no doubt in his mind that the man had seen an angel, the spirit of God, call it whatever you want; he saw him clearly, and all was alright.

Later, he was the pastor in Nashville, Illinois where Walter attended high school. Walter was on the basketball team, in a school play, and gave a comical reading at his high school graduation.

Walter's parents were assigned to a church in DeSoto, Illinois when it was time for his college years. His parents bought a Model-T Ford, which had to be cranked to start, so Walter could live at home in DeSoto and attend school at Southern Illinois Normal University (SINU) in Carbondale.

His brothers rode along and attended high school in Carbondale at Carbondale Community High School. After receiving his teaching degree (ed. note: actually it was a certificate as a degree was not required to teach at that time), Walter got a job at Glendale School north of Murphysboro. It was an eight-month job. Walter lived with Ardell and Eva Crews who did his laundry and made a lunch for him. He had about eight students, some of whom kept in contact with him until his death.

Each spring and summer Walter returned to college. In 1938 he returned full-time to college to finish his undergraduate degree, which he received in the spring of 1939.

Editor's note: The following document was written by Walter Smith in October 1989. It describes his 50th Anniversary since graduating from Southern Illinois University (SIU) and his struggles to attend college in the 1930s.

Reflections on Commuting to College by Walter

This week the SIU Class of 1939 was inducted into the "Half Century Club." As a part of the Homecoming Celebration of 1989, the Alumni Association held a banquet in our honor in the Student Union Building. The program consisted of a slide show taking pictures from the 1939 Yearbook and blending them with present day campus scenes. It was very impressive and professionally done. As the highlight of the evening, we were presented individually with "Half Century" certificates, reminiscent of graduation day.

The event brought back a flood of memories of life in the 1930s. Some class members wrote essays on college life then. They were interesting and picturesque vignettes largely from the point of view of a student who lived on campus. However, there were hundreds of us who commuted to the campus daily from the neighboring towns. What was college life in the 1930s like for them? My experience was fairly typical.

When the 1930s began, I was in the midst of my last two years of high school in Nashville, Illinois. High school was fun and easy for me. I made relatively good grades with little effort. I was in the junior and senior plays, school operettas, and was a member of the varsity basketball team those years, too. I enjoyed the class plays, the operettas, the basketball trips, etc. Our class of 1933 decided to present our own program for graduation using our own talent. We had a mixed quartet, some solos, vocal and instrumental, a valedictory speech, and I was chosen to close the program with a humorous reading.

After graduation in June 1933, college was a distant dream. During the summer following high school graduation we had a lot of family discussions about what to do. My parents were very anxious to have me go to college, but that seemed out of the question. My father was the pastor of a small Methodist church there with an annual salary of $800.

I remember that a Mr. Cliff Brown came to see me from McKendree College. He wanted me to come and offered special help for a minister's son. But, after he left, we sat down and figured that I would have to borrow at least $500 per year to attend McKendree. After graduation from college there was no guarantee of a job and, besides, our family did not borrow or buy things on credit, except for our car. It was a gloomy time for us.

In the meantime, I took a summer job on a nearby farm at $20 per month, plus room and board. I took the job because no other one was available. This job meant getting up at 4:30 a.m. working in the fields until sunset, and then literally falling into bed again. I shocked 85 acres of wheat and 45 acres of oats by myself. I then drove a bundle wagon on a threshing run of 10 or 12 farms (ed. note: in some regions, a wagon was used for hauling bundles dropped in the field by binders, and was sometimes referred to as a bundle wagon), then helped haul all of the grain to the nearest elevator about 8 miles away. This was all done with horses as there were no tractors there, tough on a "soft" small-town lad.

Toward the end of the summer, our family received some good news. My parents had not given up on my going to college, and we learned that the pastor on the DeSoto Methodist Circuit was moving and we might be stationed there. We knew that there was a teacher's college just eight miles away. Furthermore, the tuition and books cost only $10 per quarter (ed. note: the college school year was divided into "quarters" then instead of "semesters" as they are today.) While teaching school was not my vocational preference, for me it beat milking cows and shocking wheat. My parents were elated that they could send their children to college.

The summer job ended in August and in early September 1933 we moved to DeSoto. My farmer boss sold some grain and paid me $60. I was rich! I invested my money in school clothes -- a suit, a sport jacket, a pair of shoes, extra trousers, etc. and had $10 left for the fall tuition. Commuting to college was a definite possibility.

We had just one more hurdle, transportation. My father suggested that by juggling our meager budget and sacrifice, we might buy a four or five year old Model-A Ford. So, off to Vogler Ford in Carbondale we traipsed, only to learn that our dream car was not available. We did find a 1926 Model-T Ford. The salesman described it as clean, sharp, and a real beauty, priced at only $25. Now the Model-T and the Smith family were old friends. We had suffered through two or three, more than slightly used ones. We knew all of their shortcomings. They were legend! But, ah shucks, the price was right so we took a chance. I was all set for school.

All went well until the first frosty morning. She refused to start. The battery was too weak to pull the starter. This meant we must crank it by hand, no easy task. We soon learned to jack up a rear wheel and put it in gear for an easier start. But, there were more woes. The radiator leaked just enough that it would not hold antifreeze. So, every cold night we drained the radiator and jacked up a rear wheel in preparation for a faster get away the next morning. There was more. Since I was going

Walter & His Model-T

to Carbondale daily, and since DeSoto had only a two-year high school, my parents arranged for my two younger brothers to go to Carbondale Community High School. This meant planning our schedules so that three of us began and ended the day near the same hour. It wasn't always easy, but I remember no serious conflicts. I always took an 8 o'clock class to get us going early and then struggled to get my entire library studies finished by about 3:30 p.m.

Another vivid memory I have of commuting to college was my daily lunch. I had to brown bag it, of course. This meant sameness every day. I could count on one of three menus: bologna, peanut butter and jelly, or apple butter sandwiches. The worst of all were the soggy, soggy apple butter. We commuters were told that we could eat our lunches in the gymnasium. The sweaty smell of the locker room was too much for me, so I usually ate in the car.

Reflections on Commuting to College
By Walter

Needless to say, I parked on the back campus. I was embarrassed to have sophisticated students see me coaxing old "Liz" to start. I would have called her worse names, but was restrained by being a member of a minister's family. Years later I learned that some of the students envied me. At least I had wheels.

Enough on the mechanics; what about the class work? My Freshman Advisor was Emma Bowyer. Though sometimes she seemed impersonal and tough, when she grew to understand my struggle as a commuter trying to earn a teacher's certificate, she was most helpful. I was disappointed that she was not assigned to me as my advisor in my sophomore year. There were many others like Mr. Fleming Cox, Mr. Charles Pardee, Miss Elizabeth Cox, and Dr. Thomas Barton who inspired and encouraged commuters like me.

For some of my classmates, college was "fun and games," and "jellying" across the street at Carter's Café (ed. note: "jellying" is a term used in the 1930s for what we might describe today as loafing or killing time.) They could study evenings at the library. For commuters, term papers, collateral reading, and study for exams had to be done while on campus and called for much self-discipline. A trip back to the campus for evening study was too expensive. I had to follow a strict regimen and be finished by 3:30 p.m.

This brings me to our home. Our parsonage in DeSoto was the proverbial "five rooms and a path" between them. There was no central heating, no inside plumbing, no adequate lighting. Five people in this little space meant there was no place where you could get alone to read and study. The family gathered around the heating stove in the living room each evening to listen to the radio. We had good family times, but it was not conducive to studying for an 8 o'clock exam.

Still, with encouragement of parents and teachers, I earned a teacher's certificate in June 1935 (ed. note: only two years of college were needed at the time to earn a teaching certificate.) At the moment, that was as far as I could go. In those days the oldest son was expected to get a job and help his parents with some of his earnings. I was very glad to do this. Also, my brother next to me, Artie was ready for college.

That summer we had another stroke of good fortune. The Glendale rural school just north of Murphysboro needed a teacher. I heard of it early, applied, and got the job. What a thrill to be able to earn some of my own way. I took the job wondering if I would ever finish college, but determined to help out at home to repay my parents. When I received my first paycheck I traded the Model-T for a 1930 Model-A Ford, and a year later turned it over to my family for my brothers to drive to school.

During the school year 1935-36, I boarded with Ardell and Eva Crews, Monday through Friday. They lived about one mile from Glendale School. It was a one-room school, with about 16 children in 6 of the 8 grades.

It was a source of pride to have a job, though a difficult one. A rural school teacher in the 1930s was not only a teacher, but a nurse, janitor, playground supervisor, advisor to the School Board, community leader, and more. All of this was done for a salary of $65 a month. I was enormously happy when they hired me back the next year for $80 per month. The third year I asked for $85 per month and was turned down. I was told that Glendale usually changed teachers every two years, but I was so well liked that they would make an exception and hire me back if I would take it for $80. Jobs were scarce! What does one do! After pondering it for a week or so I signed on for the third year, 1937-38. The school term was just eight months which meant just eight month's pay. But, it was a job and a chance to go to college in the summer. I was determined to get my college degree.

During the 1930s SIU was very anxious to help teachers complete their college education. Each year they planned Mid-Spring Terms, six weeks, and a Summer Term, nine weeks, especially for rural teachers. I attended both Mid-Spring and Summer Terms in 1936-37-38. This constituted my third year of college.

In the spring of 1938, encouraged by my pastor, Reverend E.B. Beaty, I applied to enter the Methodist Ministry. Indeed, that did seem like the right thing for me. I was accepted and promised a student charge, the Oraville Circuit (ed. note: a "charge" is a preaching assignment), and was admitted to the Conference. This afforded me the opportunity to return to college full-time in September 1938. Ardell and Eva Crews agreed to give me room and board for $4.50 per week. I stayed with them and commuted to Carbondale daily.

Editor's note: In one of his sermons later in his life, Walter spoke of a day when it was announced that a man was flying an airplane and landing in a meadow near the SIU campus. This man was offering rides in his plane for $1.50 and Walter decided to check it out. He watched the airplane take off and land several times. When it was his turn to fly, he got in the passenger seat and looked the plane over. He decided not to go. He was a man of faith but he had no faith in that old airplane.

The school year, 1938-39 was uneventful but a very full one. I had to prepare sermons for my churches as well as carry a full load of college classes during the week. In fact, because of changes in requirements for graduation over the years, I had lost a few credits toward graduation requirements, but by carrying nineteen hours each term, I finished in June 1939.

Graduation Day, June 2, 1939. Along with a few over two-hundred others, I received a Bachelor of Education Degree. After the graduation ceremony in Shryock Auditorium, all of us spent some time in small groups out on the campus. The atmosphere was electric for all of the graduates as we congratulated each other. I remember too, standing with my diploma and admiring the buildings -- Shryock with its ornate adornment, the Old Science Hall with its interesting turrets, Old Main where I had taken the majority of my classes. The campus looked so big, the crowds of happy people everywhere. What a day!

Then it began to sink in -- I

Graduation Day, 1939

had done it. This was a new plateau that no one else in my family had ever reached. My ancestors had been in America for at least one hundred and fifty years. I had some thirty-five uncles and aunts, plus over forty first cousins, none of whom had graduated from college. Even my father, an ordained minister, was not a college graduate. It was an eerie, awesome feeling that was beyond expression. I pondered this and many other things about college and life and family and soaked up the atmosphere for more than an hour. Then, I got in my trusty car and drove home, alone with my thoughts.

HAIL, SOUTHERN, HAIL. You gave me one of the most unforgettable days of my life. HAIL!

My College Years by Emma

I remember mother encouraged me to go to college after I graduated from Christopher High School in 1938. I wanted to go to college and become a teacher. Mom sent me to the high school during the summer to talk to the principal Mr. Geoffrey Hughes about it. He had hired me to keep classroom attendance during my senior year. He had just received a notice that day that a couple, Elmer and Alice Knight in Carbondale, needed a student to live in and babysit a six year old child, and help clean up after the evening meal, clean the house on Saturdays, etc. That took care of room and board.

Tuition plus books in those days was $18.50 per quarter (ed. note: the college school year was divided into "quarters" at the time instead of "semesters" as they are today). We didn't have that, so mother cashed in Dad's insurance policy to pay for it. We also borrowed from a church fund. She took out an insurance policy (ed. note: probably whole-life insurance) at 5 cents per week to be sure we could pay back the church loan.

We paid the boy next door who was driving back and forth to Carbondale each day to take me to the Knight's house on Oak Street. Thus my college career began.

They were a very lovely family in Carbondale. The man worked at the transportation office. Joan Knight, the six-year old child, and I had twin beds in the same room and I had a desk. I put her to bed and then I studied. I took 17 quarter hours that fall and struggled with a new family, a step up in schooling with many more students than I was used to being around, and a heavier load than I needed to start with. I finished that quarter with mediocre grades. I walked to school about a mile every day.

I fell into a routine and made average grades for the next three years. I walked from Oak Street which is on the north side of town to the college on the south side of town. I took my lunch so I only had two trips each day. One day Mr. Knight said "if you will be ready so I can get to work at the Highway Department at eight, I'll take you to school." It was great to only have to walk home in rain and snow and sunshine as I went to school in summers, also.

When the Knights were promoted to the Springfield Office of Transportation, they found me a new home. The Dick Sherenty family consisted of mother, dad, and Sally, an eight year old. She didn't take much care. They decided their house on Main Street was too small for them, so they built a new one on Chautauqua Avenue. While they were building, and the old house had been sold, we lived across the street at Eve Faught's house. Eve ran the SIU Laboratory and her hobby was flowers, especially irises. It was a short stay.

They eventually introduced me to the family who lived on Cherry Street. Their daughter was in Junior High. It made for a different experience. I enjoyed living there and it was much closer to school. I worked at the Woolworth store one Christmas, though I spent most of my pay for Christmas gifts for the family.

When in College during one quarter, our Physical Ed Class was a dance class. I was so klutzy and disliked the class so much that I flunked and for one credit had to take the dumb class a whole quarter again. My coordination never has improved much, to this day.

I had very few good clothes. I had one jacket I liked very much and when I ate my lunch one day in the gym, I forgot it and never saw it again. I had a Schaeffer fountain pen which I treasured. I lost it one day and a kid in my class found and returned it to me. Before the quarter was over, I lost it again. The kid who found it bemoaned the fact that he had ever returned it to me in the first place.

I didn't graduate, but received my teacher's certificate from the normal school (ed. note: "normal" colleges were what colleges for educating teachers were called at the time) and used it many times: country school between Bondville and Seymore with seven grades, Woodlawn second grade, and lots of subbing at Lebanon, Mascoutah, Albion, and Anna, Illinois.

Later I was Conference President of the United Methodist Women and didn't have time to do anymore teaching. I served this office for five years.

Courtship and Marriage by Emma

During his senior year at SIU (1938-39), Walter attended a Baptist prayer group, which met for a short period each noon. Later, Walter was the force behind the formation of the Methodist prayer group. We had about ten of us to start and it grew rapidly. This prayer group many years later became The Wesley Foundation on campus. It exists today.

Emma & Walter

I remember meeting Walter at noonday prayer meeting on campus. My first year was his last. We were each dating other people at the time. It was during the noon hour, so we didn't spend too much time together or with others at the prayer meeting. We congregated in groups to talk, picnic, and gather at a friend's house to talk and sing. Vera and Leroy Pittman were in this group. It was a good way to make friends in a good way. We formed some great friendships, some that endure today.

Walter decided to enter the ministry as his dad had done. He joined the Methodist Episcopal Church. During his last year in college, he had a student charge at Oraville, Illinois (ed. note: a charge is an assignment of a minister to a church.) The church there no longer exists.

Makanda

Walter was assigned to Makanda, Zion, and Oak Grove churches after graduating from SIU with a bachelor's degree in 1939. He was close by SIU so he kept in contact with all of us in the prayer group. By then he and his girlfriend Wilma had split. One day he sent a note to me, delivered by a friend, asking me out. My friends were so excited for my date with Walter. They all thought he was so cute and a good match for me. I had to borrow $1 from a girlfriend from Metropolis to get my hair done. In those days $1 was a lot of money and I just didn't have it. We had many more dates and picnics with friends, etc.

I remember Walter asking me to marry him and giving me a watch, which I had never had, as an engagement gift (ed. note: Emma gave Walter a ballpoint pen). I answered "yes, but told him to be sure to ask my dad for my hand." He did and we did!

We were married in August 1941. I was 20 years old and he was 25. At church time we all went across the tracks up a few yards west of the railroad to the little church on the hill in Makanda.

We had a simple wedding ceremony after church. After Walter's dad preached the sermon, Walter and I went forward with my sister Laura and his best friend Virgil Jones and Walter's dad married us.

Both families were there as well as the church people, special friends from college, and old friends. Among them were Vera Johnson and Leroy Pittman who are still good friends.

Walter picked up my family and me and took us to his parsonage home up the hill west of the railroad that ran through the middle of the town. The business district was built along the tracks up the hill a bit. It is still the same today. Walter's brother Artie, wife, and child were also there. After the wedding we all went back to Walter's house. His mother made the group dinner there.

We went out to our car, a 1941 Ford, and saw it was all decorated with old shoes and tin cans tied to it. Our friends had rigged Walter's car with old shoes and tin cans and threw rice.

We took off for Centralia. That night we stayed in Walter's parents' house in Centralia and his parents stayed at Walter's house in Makanda. Walter's friends found us in Centralia and took Walter on a "chivaree" to celebrate the wedding (ed. note: chivalries are noisy celebrations or parties with friends and family.) They made him straddle a pole and while on it carried him down to the pond. There they jokingly threatened to toss him in while wearing his only good suit. A chivaree was a common practice in those days which is why we attempted to hideout at Walter's parent's house.

The next morning we started for Chicago on our honeymoon. It was a little hard to find a motel as there were very few in those days.

We stayed in Kankakee at a Tourist Home. One of the things we did was to go to see the Cubs play ball. We parked on the street about a block away and walked back to the park. It was my first major league game. It was an experience for both of us. Walter loved baseball and I had hardly been out of Christopher, except to school and to the zoo in St. Louis when I was a child. One didn't go far from home in those days. How different from today's weddings and honeymoons! It was all that we could afford and we were happy with it all.

That was the first of many "faraway places" he took me in our 56½ years of married life. I became addicted to travel.

He taught me many truths and helped me establish my faith. The congregations of the churches Walter served at the time -- Makanda, Zion, and Oak Grove -- gave us showers with lovely gifts and a chivaree, which was popular at the time.

Emma & Walter at the parsonage in Makanda, 1941

People in the congregations gave us chickens, helped us can peaches as this was peach country, and teased us a lot. The parsonage in Makanda was a nice two story house up a hill. The town rose up on both sides from a valley through which a train ran. Our house had a "john" that was higher up the hill from the house, as few people had indoor toilets. There was running water, a hand pump in the kitchen. Heat was obtained by coal stoves. We had a pretty one. The house is still there as it is one of the nicest houses in town, though the plumbing is undoubtedly inside now.

Walter's parents gave us a lovely living room suite and Walter had bought a nice bedroom suite. The kitchen was very sparse with no built-in cabinets. When we went to the furniture store to buy a refrigerator, etc., I heard the storekeeper talk about "carrying charges" and asked why he couldn't get a friend to deliver the furniture. I had much to learn.

Vienna

After two months of our marriage, the Conference transferred Walter from the Makanda-area churches to Vienna in 1941. He was to be paid $1,200 per year, $300 more than the previous churches. Vienna was a county seat and we "thought we had it made." Vienna Methodist Church was a hole in the ground as they were building a new church. The delegate to Conference instructed the builder that if he saw young kids around not to chase them away, that was the new pastor and his wife. A lovely new church was built that year, and opening ceremonies were held. We started the first vacation Bible school held in this church. It was wartime and the Superintendent of schools, who was in the church, asked me if I would finish teaching the school year for a teacher who had gone into defense work. I did and we then had enough money to pay off our furniture.

During these two years, Walter had taken the Conference course of studies which was required of all ministers. That didn't satisfy Walter who wanted to study and be a teacher in one of the Christian colleges.

Bondville and Farina

We moved to Bondville, west of Champaign when Walter was assigned as the minister of a church near there in 1942. We rented a house for $25 per month and I drove the car to teach school in the country between Bondville and Seymour. It had eight students in the one school, but only seven grades. Walter rode the bus to Champaign each day for classes at the University of Illinois to work on a Master's degree in religious studies.

On Sundays, we drove to a Methodist church called Mt. Vernon, north of Champaign. The congregation was so good to us. Here again, vacation Bible school was held. It was a good year.

Walter worked very hard and finished his Masters degree in religious history as he sought a teaching position at one of several religious-based colleges. However, no job opened up and he did not pursue teaching at a college much after that.

We were given a charge in Farina by the Methodist church and served there for a few months that summer. That fall, charges opened up in Methodist churches in northern Illinois, which gave Walter an opportunity to move closer to Evanston where he could further his religious education at Garrett Seminary.

Capron and Seminary

Having his Master's degree still didn't satisfy Walter, so he applied to the seminary school at Garrett on the campus of Northwestern University in 1943. No one in the family wanted him to go for the idea at the time was that seminaries were too modern in their beliefs. Walter wanted to improve himself and see both sides of the picture so he could decide for himself what he believed.

He found a two point charge in the Rock River Conference at Capron and Blaine Methodist churches just south of the Wisconsin border. Most of the people there were dairy farmers. Capron was a Norwegian town with a strong Lutheran Church. All the rest of the believers attended the Methodist Church. Those were the only two churches in town. We lived downstairs in the parsonage at Capron. It had a living room, kitchen, and utility room. The bathroom was upstairs with three unused bedrooms. The furnace was in the basement. It had to be fed coal, stoked at night, and coal ash taken out each day, but it was a good furnace.

Walter left on Mondays, as he and friends took turns driving to Garrett. Walter's roommate at Garrett was Alfonso Velasco, a pastor of Mexican descent. Walter worked in the kitchen to help with his room and board at the school. They returned to Capron on Fridays. He always brought me three or four books each week from the library.

The weekend gave Walter time to visit the sick and preach at each church. The people of the congregation often had us for dinner in the fall. After three years of this schooling, graduation was great. After we left there, the youth asked Walter to return to give their High School graduation address.

David W. Smith was born while Walter served the Capron-Blaine charges. My doctor was downtown on Michigan Avenue in Chicago. For my doctor's appointments, I rode into the city with Walter and back to Capron on the train on Monday, or took the train into the City on Friday, rode the elevated train to Evanston, and returned to Capron with Walter. David was born in Wesley Memorial Hospital near the north side of Chicago in March 1944. He was a good baby and nursed for nine months.

Kaye Smith was born the day the atom bomb was dropped in Japan. She was born in August in Belvidere, Illinois. One of the ladies in the church kept David while I was in the paternity ward of the hospital for ten days.

Walter proudly graduated from seminary in the spring of 1946. He had offers to pastor in Iowa and South Dakota. He decided to "go home" to southern Illinois to pastor for the rest of his life. We had enough of "going to the city."

Equality

We came back to southern Illinois to a pastorate at Equality, Illinois in 1946. Charles R. Smith was born in October 1947 while we were there. (ed. note: he was called "Buddy" when he was young reportedly because he was always underfoot watching and learning from what his parents and older siblings were doing.) We all went to Harrisburg, Illinois to see a parade that day. That evening I landed in the Harrisburg Hospital as that was where my doctor worked. He was a pastor's son. My nurse looked at me and said, "Didn't I see you at the parade this afternoon?" I was! The doctor said it was a near perfect birth. Everyone in Equality thought he was a beautiful baby. I did as well.

We enjoyed the two years in this little town. The beauty operator did my hair while the children had their naps across the lawn in the room with a window facing the beauty salon. It was probably the only hour I had during the day that I could use for myself once each week.

While visiting friends at Seymour, our car was stolen and wrecked. Friends at Equality loaned us a car and the church took up a donation to help defray the cost of a new one.

I often put Dave and Kaye in a playpen, but Dave soon found he could climb out and taught Kaye how. Then they took off for the neighbor's house where they had three girls who loved to play with Dave and Kaye. We had a screened in front porch where they could play freely, but they soon learned how to unlock the door and visit the neighbor girls. We put the lock up high so they got a broom and with the handle soon unlocked the door. Their mom was always busy and didn't notice for a while, so they had periods of stolen freedom.

Olney by Emma

When the Conference asked Walter if he would like to move to Olney First Methodist Church with a nice raise in salary, how could we say no! On moving day in 1948, we laid baby Buddy (Charlie) on a bench in the basement of the church and supervised the moving. The janitor came over all excited telling us, "Someone left a baby in the church basement."

The move to Olney was a great one. No one expected to "move up" so rapidly. Four years here were most productive. We had a youth group from all over town of about 30 kids. They responded to a young minister and spent many evenings at the parsonage eating popcorn and discussing ideas, asking questions and having fun. They did all kinds of activities. They started church ball teams, went to church camp, had Halloween parties, etc. Someone told me that Walter meant so much to him and that without their activities and Walter's counseling he probably would be in prison today.

Five boys went into the ministry. They included John Cox, Boyd Wagner, Lavon Baylor, and Ralph Totten. Several girls went into nursing. One older girl, Barbara Campbell, became a deaconess. Our "sleeping children" upstairs hated to leave all of the joviality. They probably spent more time on the stairway listening than their parents realized.

When David started kindergarten, we hated to see him "leave the nest" for a day. The children had a sandbox in the backyard and spent a lot of time with friends from down the street. They also had an invisible friend called "Uncle Eddie" that they played with.

Olney's house was old and large. We had four bedrooms, so mom, dad, and baby Charlie got one room. Later Charlie moved into Dave's room with a twin or bunk bed. Kaye had her own room and the extra room was used as a playroom. The kids used imagination and turned chairs over to build a train, a card table covered with a sheet to make a circus tent, etc. They had lots of other toys and once each month all was gathered into a bushel basket and taken to the attic and the basketful from the former month was brought down. This made the toys seem new to them as they hadn't played with them for a long time.

We read every day before naptime. Each week we visited the library and each one picked out the books they wished for me to read to them that week. Some were chosen several times. As the family multiplied this tradition "hit the rocks" for mom didn't have or took the time to read to the children, and they didn't seem to want to read to each other. The "Little Golden Books" and records took up a lot of time. They could hear the records, read, and sing as they followed along in their books. "The Little Red Hen" and "Porky Pig" were a few of the other books. I'm surprised I've forgotten the names of other books, we heard them so often.

I remember at Olney having a man come to the door to see Walter. Walter was calling on the parishioners, as he did each weekday afternoon, so I invited the man in to wait for Walter's return. I visited with him for a bit and then had to start supper. The man asked if he could watch me fix the meal, so I invited him back to the kitchen. Walter returned and they talked. When the man left Walter told me that the man had just been released from prison where he was a cook, thus the interest in my preparing food. He had spent most of the money he was given since his release and needed a job. Walter sent him to Robinson, Illinois where the refinery needed cooks. We could not open our house today as we did then. We had many such experiences.

We had a very successful ministry in Olney. They welcomed a young family and responded well to Walter's ministry there.

Editor's note: While serving in Olney, Walter was approached by the Methodist Bishop to promote and expand participation in the camp meeting in Louisville, Illinois.

Epworth Camp by Walter

As a background to these remarks let me speak briefly about the camp meeting (ed. note: a camp meeting is a religious revival held for several days usually in a rural setting.) I have heard that under the direction of local Methodist pastor in Louisville, a group of men got together and formed the Clay County Holiness Association. I think that this occurred either in the late 1920s or the 1930s. They began holding a summer camp meeting using a large tent to house the services.

The Holiness Association grew in popularity and support through the years. It was in an era when there were a number of thriving camp meetings in southern Illinois. In addition to Eldorado, there were Tilden, Bonnie and Jacob's Camp just to name a few. At the close of World War II when material and manpower became available, the Clay County Holiness Association bought a piece of property on the northern edge of Louisville and built a sizeable tabernacle. As I recall, they also built a small book store and office, plus two small "workers" cabins.

It was about this time that the camp was at its peak. Some of the Board of Directors, wanting to increase its mission and service, went to the Methodist District Superintendent, Dr. Earl C. Phillips and asked him to establish a Summer Youth Institute using the Camp facilities free of charge.

Dr. Phillips had been a former Dean of the Eldorado Institute, so he saw the possibilities of such a project in the Olney District. He sought the support of several pastors in his district and the project was begun. A small but enthusiastic group met for a summer camp. I think that was either 1947 or 1948.

In 1948, I was appointed to the Olney First Methodist Church. A few months later, Dr. Phillips came to me soliciting my help in leading and promoting his youth project. I remember that he wanted to pattern it after the Eldorado Institute which was such a huge success in the southern part of the Conference.

Our Olney Church had a large two-story cabin at Eldorado, and our youth had been encouraged to attend the Eldorado Camp by my predecessor, Dr. H.E. Burge. Naturally, I hesitated to change what appeared to be a successful and popular program.

However, it soon became evident that the new camp in Louisville could accomplish the same mission and that we in the Olney Church were needed to assure its success. So, I encouraged our church to sell its Eldorado cabin and build a new one at Louisville.

In the meantime, a plot of ground, about seven acres, became available for purchase adjoining the Holiness Camp grounds on the east. It had been the estate of one of Louisville's more affluent citizens, who had since died and his ancestors had neglected it. There was a large two-story house on the acreage which was in poor repair. This old house was used as a girl's dormitory for several years. Dr. Phillips seized the opportunity and raised the necessary funds to buy the property for the Olney District. He wanted the Camp to have a decided Methodist flavor so he named it the Epworth Methodist Youth Institute of the Olney District.

Having sold our Eldorado property, the Olney Church built the first institute cabin on the new property. Flora Methodist Church followed us promptly, as did Clay City and several others. The Camp grew at a rapid pace.

At about this same time Dr. Phillips urged me to take his place in leadership as Dean of the Institute. So, I guess that I was the first official Dean of Epworth Youth Institute. Our immediate concern was a dining hall where safe nutritious meals could be prepared and served. We had been using a large tent as a make-shift dining room.

Dr. Phillips raised the funds in a very short time and we spent some $10,000 building and furnishing the new dining space. We built it on Methodist owned property, of course. About this time we heard of a small Church college in Springfield, Missouri that was closing and selling its properties. We learned that it had a good supply of stainless steel serving trays, stainless tableware, as well as a good supply of pots and pans. So, early one spring morning Rev. Gerald Gulley, who was the Louisville pastor, and I took my car and went to Springfield. We found the church College and loaded my car to the roof with our kitchen supplies.

At about this same time, we asked some of our farmers to come with their plows and tractors and level off a spot large enough for a softball diamond. The new facilities made Epworth Institute more popular than ever, so it grew quickly to near capacity.

We were now ready to carry out our programs of classes in churchmanship in the morning, recreation in the afternoon and most important of all, strong evangelistic service each evening.

In 1952, I became District Superintendent of the Olney District. I continued to promote the Epworth Institute in all our churches. In those days I visited each charge three or four times per year and was able to know a great number of our laity, including the youth. I continued as Dean for another year or so then turned the

Ringing the Bell

leadership over to others. I am not sure, but I believe that Rev. Max Martin, the pastor at Flora, became my successor.

My interest in Epworth continued throughout my term as District Superintendent and onward, but after leaving the district in 1958, I gradually lost contact and have little recollection of the later history of Epworth Camp. I do know that over the years many young people found a deep Christian experience there and some responded to the call to preach through the services of Epworth Youth Institute.

Editor's note: The Epworth Youth Institute was closed in 2015. The following is a tribute written by Tim Price in his online blog entitled *"Turning Out the Lights at Epworth Camp."*

Epworth Camp by Tim Price & Others

About three months ago now, I helped lead worship for the final Epworth Camp Service in Louisville, Illinois. It was the end of an era. The spirit was upbeat, people were grateful and thankful and there was a vision for something new, which I think is always helpful.

Reflecting back to the last time I left an actual camp meeting at Epworth -- it was at the close of Holiness Camp in mid-July of 2015. The final service of the final camp of the season ended about 8:30 on Sunday evening, we packed up the sound system, loaded the Harvest trailer and then talked to a few people for a bit. Then, I walked back in to the dining hall all by myself, shut off the lights, walked out, got in the van and drove off. That was it. I still remember the interesting sense of finishing.

After a quick calculation, including summer camps and other weekend events, it looks like I've spent about 380 nights at Epworth Camp in Louisville. This number is topped only by Beulah Camp, which I have attended since I was an infant. When a person has been somewhere for more than a year, if you stacked all those nights end to end, it does begin to feel like home in some way.

Epworth opened up in 1947 as a dream of a pastor in the area who wanted a camp in close geographical proximity. Times have changed and people do drive farther for things these days -- so the geographical issue may not be as a big of deal as it once was. But for 68 years, this dream has been alive -- to reach students in that part of the world for Christ.

My first summer was 1992. That would mean I've been connected there for 23 years -- 35% of the camp's total history! My mom was also a camper there when she was a teenager. That's pretty amazing history.

Most all the Harvest people over the last 20 years have passed by Epworth Camp in one way or another. There were some Harvest team members, who after serving went on to serve in ministry at Epworth -- on the core teams or as speakers and leaders. Here are some of the highlighted Harvest and Epworth memories:

1. It was one of the first Senior High Camps to invite me to lead music for the week -- just me and the guitar.

2. It was one of the first week-long camps for which Harvest led worship, even before Harvest was named Harvest.

3. I remember playing the guitar for hour and twenty minutes one evening during an altar call time at Epworth. Later that fall, after that summer evening worship service, I recorded *Altar*, an instrumental prayer album. I have always gotten comments about this music.

4. Of all the camps Harvest has served, there have been more ER trips at Epworth than any other -- thankfully all relatively minor.

5. Camping has always been a very hands on opportunity for many folks -- including me. God used Epworth in lots of faith journeys!

Editor's note: After Mr. Price wrote his tribute above, the following testimonies were added to his online blog by various former attendees of the camp.

By Heather, January 2016: I went to Epworth with my grandma and grandpa Rolland Devor. They had all of us grandkids with them. It was so much fun. I will never forget all the songs and stories and all the late night's talking about how much fun we had that day. I miss camp, I miss my grandpa, and I will never forget all the memories we made there.

By Yvonne, January 2016: I remember going to church camp at Epworth in Louisville when I was 10 years old until I was 16. My mom, Betty Mulvany worked in the kitchen. Back then the hill didn't bother me, but boy I tried it when we had a family reunion on top of the hill. They even built new dorms. I hate to see them shut it down. I have good memories there. I met a lot of good friends there. All the good times we all had. We came from Xenia United Methodist Church and we had a lot from there. That's when we had the two-story cabins. New dorms weren't even talked about then.

###

By Steve, January 2016: I was on Core Staff at Epworth for 6 years while I was on staff at First UMC in Olney. Worked with Brad Henson and Leroy Allison to put together the senior high camp and loved spending that week with the young people each summer. I was there the first year Tim Price came to lead the music. Great memories of seeing the Lord work in the hearts of many young men and women.

By Ron, January 2016: I went to Epworth camp as a teenager and got saved. I came back later as a young adult and served as a camp dorm leader and teacher, and back again as the camp nurse where Tim Price was the song leader. I believe Tim's first year. I had lots of good memories. Seen young people get saved, healed, and delivered.

By Alan, June 2016: My history with Epworth dates from infancy as I grew up in Louisville. My dad, Royal Erwin was the treasurer for the Holiness Camp Association which owned the tabernacle and surrounding grounds. Southern Illinois Conference owned the back part of the property from the dining hall on up the hill including the 2-story "cabins" and the large house at the east end of the property. The Louisville church would dismiss local worship and attend Holiness Camp during the two weeks it was in session. This was followed with two weeks of "youth camp", one for junior high and one for senior high.

The ringing of the large bell always told people around town when breakfast was served, morning worship, time for lunch, 2 o'clock worship for Holiness Camp, evening meal time, and 7 o'clock worship. This went on for three weeks in the summer for years and years.

I worked as part of the music staff for several years for Holiness Camp and for senior high camp by playing a spinet Hammond organ on loan from a music dealer in Effingham in the mid 1960's -- early 1970's. In the 1950-1965-era there were such large crowds for Holiness

Camp and Epworth that wooden folding chairs had to be brought from storage and put outside the tabernacle on both sides, and large canvas meeting tents were set up around the grounds for Bible study and other classes during Epworth.

###

<u>Editor's note</u>: While living in Olney, Walter and Emma had an opportunity to visit Europe and the Holy Land in the fall of 1951. The following are their memoirs and letters written while they were travelling there. The trip itinerary, prepared by American Express Travel Services, is interspersed throughout these writings in order to show the timeline of the trip. After Emma's introduction, the first letter written below is from Emma's brother Carl, written from Paris where he was living at that time.

Please note that their memoirs are in <u>block paragraphs</u>, correspondence is in *italics*, and trip itinerary and comments are preceded with the phrase "<u>Editor's note</u>" or "<u>ed. note</u>."

Introduction by Emma

Walter had been saving for 10 years and was owed two months' vacation while we were in Olney. He asked the church Board if he might go to the Holy Land and they consented. A parishioner, Mrs. Caen, asked me if I could go along if she gave me the money. Plans were made for the grandparents to come and stay with the children while we were away.

We went to Europe and spent a month there and went to the Holy Land and spent a month there. We were gone two months. We sailed to Southampton, England on the Queen Elizabeth. I got sick on the ocean.

Essentially, people in other lands are just like us. They work hard, raise families, love and are loved, and worship something or someone. As we visit each country, I should like to point out a few personality and background differences.

<u>Editor's note</u>: Emma's additional memoirs are interspersed throughout with the travel itinerary and letters to and from the couple.

Letter from Carl Lutes

August 24, 1951
Paris, France

Dear Em and Walt,

Well, I guess by now you're aboard and on your way. I hope you like the ocean and the travel. Personally, I love it. I am looking forward to my trip home. Relax and enjoy yourself and have a nice time, for you'll be busy every minute after you arrive on the continent. I don't think you'll get sick -- I never was. It's mostly mental.

I have decided that I will go to London. So don't be surprised if you see me show up. I will probably get there about the 5th of September. At any rate, I will write you the details later at American Express in England. If I can stretch my money enough I may come back through Holland and Belgium with you. I won't be able to take the tours and stay in the rich Hotels, etc., but I can see you on the trip, anyway.

I hope you brought the movie camera, as there will be many things that a still camera just won't capture, and no bigger than it is to carry, it is really wonderful to have along.

Mom's package finally came yesterday, so I'm stuffing myself with candy bars today. I was really glad to get it, but the summer clothes are a little late. It's really rather chilly here.

I also got a nice long letter from Jim. He seems rather happy but anxious for his furlough (<u>ed. note</u>: his brother Jim was in the military at the time.)

I hope you don't get stuck in too many restaurants where they sell liquor, but I'm sure you will often; so just prepare yourself for it. Just tell them you want milk or coffee and forget everybody else, because they know that Americans often don't drink.

I think you should be careful in wearing slacks, Em. In certain countries they don't like them. In England and on the ship I'm sure they'll be wonderful and everybody will wear them, but I'm not so sure of the Eastern counties and Holland. In France they aren't too common.

Oh, yes, there's one more thing. Don't expect to be liked too much in England, as they don't exactly adore Americans. They're so jealous because their country is about to go under and they don't have anything to eat, etc., while Americans have everything.

Well, bon voyage, and don't eat too much or fall overboard. I'll probably see you about the 5ᵗʰ. I'll write you in London before I come. Take it easy, Carl

Letter from Walter's Mother

August 28, 1951
Olney, Illinois

Dear mother and daddy,

Well here it is Tuesday night and all is well and fine. Kaye says are you better and David says I hope you are well and Granddad and Grandma says hoping you are having a nice trip. It is now 9 o'clock and Buddy is fast asleep. Just finished David's story and am going to read one for Kaye.

Sam had a good sermon Sunday night and a good crowd. His subject was "Prepare the Way for the Lord."

The children register for school Tuesday the 4ᵗʰ. Kay's cost is $5.20 and David is $4.80.

We made a little trip out to Mt. Erie and Johnsville then back to this Clay County home. We had rain Sunday night and again today. We washed but the clothes are still hanging in the basement. So, if the sun comes up tomorrow, I shall hang them outside.

*David says not too much else to tell you so we say good
night and hope you sleep well. As ever, David, Kaye, Buddy,
Granddad, and Grandma. See you in November.*

P.S. -- received the telegram this morning.

<u>Editor's note</u>: On Tuesday, August 28, Walter & Emma embarked on
the S.S. Queen Elizabeth of the Cunard White Star Line at Pier 90
in New York City. It sailed at 12:01 a.m. on August 29 and arrived
at Southampton, England on Monday, September 3. Their travel to
London was by train. The following are letters by Walter and Emma.

September 4, 1951
London, England

Dear David, Kaye, Bud, and Grandma,

> *How I wish you might have been along with us to see the
ship pull out of New York harbor. The skyline was lovely and
we had a good look at the Statue of Liberty. Hope our picture
turns out well.*
> *The ship itself is so nice and so large. The food is good.
I feel light-headed all of the time, but considering having been
sick and the motion of the ship, one can expect that.*
> *Our cabin is very tiny, but we hardly do more than sleep
and wash there. Most of our time, we spend in the reading room
or on the top of the ship where there are chairs and cushions to
sit and enjoy the travel of the ship.*
> *Someday we want you all to come to New York and see
for yourself all these things.*
> *The ship is full of English, more than Americans. We like
them very much. Most of them have very little of anything and
are nice about it. They've been visiting relatives in America or
working in Canada and are glad to get back.*

I had very little trouble with my stomach coming over. The riding so much in the car nauseated me though.

We stopped in Washington, D.C. and saw the Washington, Lincoln, and Jefferson Memorials; the White House, Senate and House of Representatives building, treasury, Tomb of Unknown Soldier, and Capitol building.

David, we ate chop suey in Washington and the people who cooked and served it were Chinese. We sure would like to see you guys. Be good and mind Grandma. Have her write and tell us who your teachers are and all about school. Has "Bud" coaxed Grandma to buy a bulb for his snowman yet?

In Philadelphia we saw Independence Hall, Betsy Ross' home, Quaker Meeting House, and Christ Church. Love, Daddy and Mother

The British by Emma

The Queen Elizabeth was filled with Britishers, whom we observed and enjoyed. Most of them were as glad to return to England from the United States and Canada as we were to return to our ancestral land. Everyone had food parcels bought in the U.S. Even the ship itself bought supplies in New York for the round trip. England still had rationing for the seven years since World War II and the average person yearned for good food. We met them everywhere we went onboard as they return from "holiday" in the U.S.

People we contacted onboard our ship were a Scottish teacher; a teacher of Chemistry from Blackpool, England; Jewish people traveling to England from Canada to visit relatives in England; a Belgian lady saying goodbye to her son; and two ladies and a boy from Cape Town, South Africa.

We met Carl in London and then went to Belgium, Holland, and France with him. We went around London then crossed the channel to Belgium. We were happy to see a face that we knew.

The Britishers were an extremely proud people, always socially correct, but we found that once this ice was broken they were friendly, helpful, and as fair-minded as any people we have ever met. They often put the snobbish American travelers to shame.

Any other country would have given in after as much bombing as London alone took during the War, but the British seemed to have a stamina all their own. Maybe that is why they're called "Johnny Bulls." We admired them a great deal.

Women in England worked as ticket takers on buses and street cars. English women were quite "nil" in comparison to the women of some of the other countries we visited, but perhaps if we had been through all they had been through during the War we might radiate a bit less.

The men and boys all wore shirts, ties, and coats all of the time. The shirt often was frayed at the collar, the coat patched and the tie hung like a rag, but they all wore them never the less. Children here wore short pants until they were of College age. Walter found his sport clothes very much out of place and my dresses a bit bright.

The British love their king and queen, and never seem to criticize them.

They are very slow to change. That is why perhaps, they have so many lovely old buildings. We would tear them down in our country and erect something modern in their place.

An American started a department store, Harrods, in London and revolutionized shopping in that city -- then the country. They now have lovely shopping places, but to get the best goods, one must buy in the export department and have the articles sent to their ship or back home. Trade was needed so badly by the British that the best of everything was exported and they do with the lesser goods, such as woolens, china, etc. There were only utility brands left for the Britishers to buy. They told us that women whose good china was broken in air raids during the War could not have them replaced at all as the good china was shipped abroad to be sold.

Each house and apartment had window boxes of bright flowers. Roofs were often made of thatch.

The English always offered tea. We were invited to tea in London by a Methodist minister's wife. Their son was a vegetarian because they had no meat during the War and he had not learned to like it.

September 8, 1951

Train from London to Harwich, England (ed. note: written on stationery from the Waldorf Hotel in London and address to Walter's mother.)

Dear Mom,

We're on a train leaving London to Harwich, then by steamer to Hook of Holland. We didn't have nearly enough time in England. We liked it very much. We are fine, but tired. We lost your second letter to London before we even read it. It's so much hurry and scurry and so many details. It is fun though. Love all the kiddies extra hard for us. We miss them most on Sundays. Walter and Emma

Editor's note: Saturday, September 8, they left London by train to Harwich, boarded steamer to Holland, then boarded train to Hotel Krasnapolski in Amsterdam. They left for Hotel des Colonies in Brussels on September 10.

Holland and Belgium by Emma

Carl was studying in Paris and met us in London and accompanied us to Belgium, Netherlands, and Paris. He showed us the French city. From there we went on alone to Switzerland where we loved the Alps, Italy, and Greece.

We found the people of Holland to be plain, informal, friendly, very clean, blonde, and with fat babies. Whole families bicycled together. Their youth gathered at night and went down the street singing together. They loved music. A woman might get whistled at. The native dress was worn in Volendam, Holland. The people in Holland were mostly protestant. We visited a church in New Kirk on a Sunday where three-quarters of the congregation were youths. This was where the Dutch Queen was crowned.

The people of Belgium were half French and half Dutch. We had very little social connections with the Belgians. Downtown Brussels was lovely.

September 11, 1951
Hotel des Colonies
Brussels, Belgium

Dear Folks, kiddies too,

We saw Brussels this morning. It is nice, but London is so much nicer that we were not too impressed. The people here are part Dutch and part French.

Today is Carl's birthday. We just had milk, pastries, and fruit in our room for lunch, but are taking Carl out to eat tonight. We have had a good time together. He and Walt have a lot of jokes at my expense. He is getting pretty homesick, but plans to stay at least until spring.

We don't like the food here very well. We never did like to eat out very well and it's hard to choose a place that is inexpensive, yet has food to one's liking. We find it hard to get water to drink. They think we're a bit simple when we ask for it and don't take liquor of some sort. Almost never find a place to eat where no hard drinks are sold, no cafeterias at all here. Walter and Emma

Editor's note: Wednesday, September 12. They left Brussels for Hotel France et Choiseul in Paris.

France by Emma

France was mostly Catholic. There was finesse there possessed by no other people I know. To me, it was overdone, but should be recognized. They wore their clothes exceedingly well. I felt like a stick the whole time I was there, with no shape at all.

Carl Lutes & Emma at a European Flea Market, 1951

Most of the French women die their hair and wear heels of quite a height. To me, they looked old before they should, however. No women keep their youthful looks like the American women. Perhaps the answer is a statement made by a French lady to my brother when she was urging him to be sure to get a French wife to take home with him. She said, "American women are spoiled and don't make good wives. Get a French girl. They know how to work." I resented the statement, yet it was food for thought for a fella told my husband the same thing on the ship coming home. He lived in New York, but had just been to Italy to marry, saying, "The Italian girls don't always seek something to entertain, they know how to work."

In France, the men keep their women subservient while they "play around." French people shop each day for their groceries, especially milk, bread, fruit, and meat.

Many French people who have bathrooms in their homes still use the "public restrooms." Restrooms on the street were wooden sheds. An individual's legs and feet could be seen. Often the children would stop on the street and pee in public. In the hotel there were no tubs, but there were bidets, low basins for washing (ed. note: think of the bidet in the first *Crocodile Dundee* movie). The French gardens were formal and very lovely.

Walter was all worked up about paying all those tips. Everywhere we went you had to pay a tip.

He had to figure out how much a 10 percent tip was. It was a different experience for us. We went to the flea market and got brass candlesticks. One was bent a little bit and had to be fixed. We got them for a good price. They were probably nineteenth century French. Bus straightened the bent one out with an anvil and hammer. They are nice and very heavy (ed. note: many of these observations were written some years later. Bus is Emma's brother-in-law.)

September 16, 1951
Hotel de France and Choiseul
Paris, France

Dear Folks,

>*Paris is lovely -- parks, flowers, buildings and all. We have nearly walked our legs off, but have seen most everything. We went to Versailles today and saw the palace and hall of mirrors where World War I peace was signed.*
>
>*Remind us to tell you how Carl lives, etc. when we return. We shall have so much to tell I may forget it.*
>
>*How is school? Hope Bud gets his nap everyday as soon as lunch is over so he can go to school next year. Love, Walter and Emma*

Editor's note: They proceeded by train on September 17 from Paris to Basile, Switzerland, went through customs, and then changed trains to Lucerne and Hotel Rutli.

On the Train by Emma

We left Carl in France and went on to Italy by train. On the train we met Belgian fellows who would keep the train windows up on a hot day, two ladies and a boy from Africa, workers on the train and in a flea market who were retired from Versailles, missionaries in an American Church in Paris who were studying in Europe, and Austrian children with Swiss Red Cross workers.

Europe and the Holy Land
By Walter, Emma, & Others

September 17, 1951

French Countryside (ed. note: written on stationery from Hotel de France and Choiseul)

Dear Folks,

We are riding along on a train, doing some writing, going to Lucerne, Switzerland. It is a nice day, somewhat cloudy, but quite comfortable.

Yes, go ahead and pay the insurance when you have the money. It will be best to send a money order or bank draft.

When it gets cool have Mr. Edmiston build a fire. He knows about it.

It is now evident that we can't get home for the first Sunday in November. Have Mr. Cramer contact Brother Magill at Lawrenceville to preach that morning and he will probably take care of the service himself in the evening, Mr. Cramer, I mean. Best to you -- Walter

Editor's note: Monday, September 17, they arrived at Hotel Rutli in Lucerne.

Switzerland by Emma

In Zurich, we met Martha Hansrudi's mother and father (ed. note: an American immigrant's parents); a hostel run by youth; American girls who rode the train down to Italy with us; and a man named Vini who was in the U.S. Navy stationed at Naples and was homesick.

Switzerland was beautiful. The Alps graced the country. Switzerland has freedom of worship; about half of them were Catholic and half protestant. We think this was one reason the people were so much more progressive for where religion is in power; it controls even people's thoughts. We visited the World Federation of Churches and World Council of Churches.

We visited a Swiss banker who, with his son, spoke English. His wife did not. The family showed us where to buy good watches for about one-third the price. They all had very expensive watches, but they had no refrigerator. We had a refrigerator, but no expensive watches.

September 20, 1951
Switzerland

Dear Grandma, Grandpa, David, Kaye, and Buddy,

We spent all day yesterday in the mountains. We ate lunch at 8,000 feet above sea level. It was as cold as January at home. Snow was everywhere.

We saw the Rhone Glacier which was ice formed there during the ice ages. It is as large as half a city block. Walt says it probably was formed just after the mountains were made.

We go up into the mountains again this afternoon. We see lots of small and large waterfalls rushing down the mountainside.

Have the children ask Miss Fletcher at the library to tell them the story of William Tell when they get the card I'm sending with his picture on it.

The girl from Israel sent these stamps for David. She is sending coins to the house. Put them away for Bud when he gets older and a birthday gift for Kaye. Walter and Emma.

Editor's note: They left Lucerne by motor coach for Hotel Mont Fleuri in Montreux on Friday, September 21. They left Montreux and entered Italy at Domodossola, then on to Hotel Touring in Milan on Sunday, September 23.

Europe and the Holy Land
By Walter, Emma, & Others

September 23, 1951
Milan, Italy

Dear Grandma, Grandpa, David, Kaye, and Buddy,

We lived on a mountain in Montreux, Switzerland. We had to go up to our hotel from the town on a small railway. The youngsters would have loved it. We were on the second floor and had a large balcony just off our room where we could sit and see the lake. We went over, around the lake, to Geneva and saw the World Council of Churches and the monuments to John Calvin and John Knox, then to see the United Nations building.

Today we came to Milan, Italy. Tomorrow we shall go to see the Leonardo Di Vinci painting of The Last Supper. We then go to Venice where part of our trip is by Gondola, a little boat that looks like that (ed. note: included a hand-drawn picture of one.) *The houses, hotels, and all are on the water all over town.*

Hope all is going well. Glad to get your letters and the children's drawings. They make us homesick, though.

Mom said to call her at the Lutes' in Christopher if you should need her as the children are more important than her job. They won't fire her as they need her too badly.

David and Kaye start your "3" like the "2" and they won't be backward.

We read our bulletin this 5 p.m., we are 7 hours ahead of you, testament and prayed. That was church time in Olney this morning.

Glad Kaye's teacher is Mrs. Cowan and I know David will like Mrs. Gallaher too.

Do they go to the library every other Saturday and get library books to read? They really keep you busy, don't they?

Our love to all and lots of love and kisses to David xoxoxo, Kaye xoxoxo, Buddy xoxoxo. I shall give daddy some for you. We are looking for mail at Rome. It is a week yet until we get there. Love and prayers, Walter and Emma

Italy by Emma

Italy was about 98% Catholic. They married at an older age than in the U.S., with the men usually marrying around age 35 and having a good job, where in the U.S. we marry early and build a life together. In Italy, men were usually greeted first -- women were just an afterthought. The

Emma with an Ox Cart Driver, 1951

Communist Party was quite strong there, as it was in France. The poorer classes hate the U.S. since we're capitalists.

We visited Saint Peter's Basilica and marveled at the Swiss Guards. We visited the breath-takingly beautiful Isle of Capri.

We met several people whose life dream was to go to the U.S. One was a former prisoner of war during World War II living in Venice.

We were told by many people in Europe that the destiny of the world lies in the hands of the U.S. Ignorance and superstition abound in this country. Yet, it was the most interesting of all countries we visited.

Roman civilization was once so great and much of the physical evidence still remains, though the people have gone backwards, almost as far as civilization can go. It seems to be rotten on the inside. Was there a warning here? Can the Church and church people get too fanatic on their stand against immorality?

We ate a lot of different foods that year. I think the best was in Italy at a hotel. Dessert was a great big bowl of fresh fruit, and I love fruit.

We met Dr. and Mrs. Fabio; Dr. and Mrs. Lordi, Methodist ministers from Italy, the latter who moved to England; Rudophia and Chauffeur; and Bishop Marston, the father-in-law of J. Montiveiler.

Editor's note: Tuesday, September 25, they left Milan, had lunch in Verona, then on to Hotel Principe in Venice. They left Venice on Thursday, September 27 by rail for Hotel Berchielli in Florence. They left Florence on Saturday, September 29 with a stopover in Perugia for lunch and arrived at Hotel de la Ville in Rome.

More on Italy by Emma

We visited several places in Italy; Florence, Venice, and Rome. We were in Rome more days than was usual. There are a lot of things to see in Rome. We didn't feel safe in Italy.

The Cathedrals in Europe were magnificent, but there were no seats. Everyone had to stand to worship and there was no heat or air conditioning. In most of Europe, the smartest children were cared for in schools, the rest were left alone. Music and athletics were sought out in the children. They were often shown little kindness. Most towns in Europe were resort areas and were fitted to cater to tourists.

There was no refrigeration anywhere in Europe. We had to go to the bars to get ice even in the best of hotels. People go all over the neighborhood for groceries. Meat was hung in doorways. There were horse's heads for sale in shops selling horsemeat.

October 1 or 2, 1951 (ed. note: the date was written as shown)
Rome, Italy

Dear Folks and Children,

We had a wonderful day in Rome yesterday. The head of the British Methodist work in Italy showed us around. He loved doing it and we got so much out of it for he knew it from a Christian and protestant angle.

We received 10 to 15 letters here at Rome and really enjoyed them. It seemed we dreaded being away another month and although the letters made us homesick, we can go on now with new vigor.

I'm glad the children are doing nicely. They will have to get acquainted with us all over again when we get home. There should be a picture of us in the top drawer in a box in the guest room. Better get it out when "Bud" is asleep or lock the door afterwards for he will investigate for himself later.

We went to an Italian Methodist Church Sunday. There are three or four here. We couldn't understand a word, but worshipped with them anyway.

Our hotel here is very nice. The nicest we're had. The food is excellent, though very expensive. We eat at cheaper restaurants most of the time.

We fly to Cairo on Wednesday, tomorrow, at 2:45 p.m. It takes a little over 6 hours.

We heard from Mrs. Cowan and she says that the children are well cared for in school. The Cowan's are very common and eat anything. You will enjoy them. The children do. They gave us $50 for our trip and they didn't have it to give any.

Daddy hasn't had his hair cut since he left home. He needs it too. We don't stop long enough to catch our breath -- there is so much to see and we don't want to miss anything.

We must go down for breakfast. Two things I insist on; early to bed and take time for breakfast (<u>ed. note</u>: she still does.)

Give the children lots of kisses for us. We get so lonely for them when we see every child around us and we'll try to make it up to them. Tell them to study at school so they will have lots to tell us, and get lots of sleep so their bodies will be able to learn and stay healthy.

Hope all is well, Love, Walter and Emma, Daddy and Mother

Editor's note: They left Rome by airplane on Wednesday, October 3 for Hotel Metropolitan in Cairo.

Egypt by Emma

From Italy we flew to Cairo, arriving at midnight on a day when it was 99 degrees. The airport had windows, but no glass or screens. In each window stood a man, wearing draped clothing and fey. By-passers watched us come and go. It was an eerie feeling.

The Sultan had dancing girls with him at the airport. We got to see those dancing girls. We were whisked away to the hotel in the City.

Walter & Emma, 1951

We were told that when you go to the airport be careful. Only take a cab that is a Mercedes and only if there is someone there to take your name. This was because people had been disappearing. They would get into a "cab" and were never heard from again. However, the Egyptians were nice to us.

Egypt is a Muslim country in which men wore gowns, turbans, fez, and have bare feet. The women wore black robes with black or multicolored masks over their faces. Their faces, when one could see under or through the veil, was almost always old and haggard looking. Partly, I would say, caused by hard circumstances under which they live and partly due to the hot rays of the sun and reflection of these rays, as Cairo is built on desert sand. This dress and old looks pertain to the common person, but even the rich, who are supposed to be among the most beautiful women in the world, age and harden early. The American women hold their age better than any nation we observed.

We stayed at the American University. Teachers from the American University entertained us one evening and took us to the flea market.

In Egypt we met a tourist cop, U.N. border guards, Y.M.C.A secretary, accountant with his wife and son at American University in Cairo, Coptic minister Fareed who was a Moslem, Baptist minister and his wife, and Jordanian doctor and his wife.

Egypt is a county of ignorance, superstition, extreme poverty, and filth. There are two classes of people living in Egypt -- the very poor and the very rich. There are few in between. The only middle class we could find was those people that the Christian church had touched and taught how to make a living, perhaps one percent of the population. The rest of the middle class were whites from England or America who do the managing and hiring of the natives for a small pittance. We saw no native leadership or management.

We saw the poor living in any kind of hovels: junk piles with tin made into a shelter, in the "city of the dead," or asleep on the street in front of our hotel. Scores of children had trachoma, in fact Fielding, in his book on travel, said that 1 in 8 in Egypt are blind or semi-blind from a childhood disease of the eye. Flies and mosquitoes are rampant. The natives just brush off the flies and don't try to kill them. There are no screens even in the best hotels, only shutters to keep out the sun. The countryside isn't any better than I have pictured it and some people could tell worse things. We were glad that we had every one of our shots that we had taken before traveling and wished we were home to find more types of inoculations to take. We dared not touch anything and ate only at the hotel or some fancy place, and then crossed our fingers that we would not get sick.

In spite of all this poverty, we saw the most beautiful and modern architectural designs of any city we have ever seen.

Labor was extremely cheap and sand was plentiful. Many of the workers -- porters in both hotels and on the railroad and waiters in restaurants -- often came from the lower Sudan to work in the cities, leaving their families behind them and return for a few days to visit perhaps once every two years.

Walter & Emma in Egypt, 1951

A trip to the pyramids and the museum to see King Tut artifacts were high lights of the trip. At Giza, we rode camels around the pyramids. Camels have little fat and their bones hurt.

The largest, or Pyramid of Cheops, has enough blocks to build a four foot wall all of the way around France. 3,000 years ago when it was built as a burial place for the pharaoh, it was covered on the outside with solid alabaster, a snow-white mineral ground into a plaster. It has since been removed to the Muhammad Ali Mosque in Cairo. The second pyramid was smaller and covered with limestone. In front of this second pyramid lies the Sphinx as though to guard it. A third, smaller pyramid and the temple where the bodies were taken to be cleansed before burial also have been unearthed and stand out on the desert with the rest.

In the National Museum in Cairo, we saw among mummies and articles of early civilization the articles from the famous King Tut tomb. It is the latest to be uncovered and was the most complete of all the found tombs, as it had not been pillaged. In this exhibit we saw baked bread, jars of water, perfume, carriages, and gold coverings for his fingers.

The Mosques, which are the temples of the Mohammedans, cover Cairo, being in number about 400. We saw the priests wind their way up the steps of the minarets five times each day to call the people to prayer. When we visited them, we had to remove our shoes or walk in canvass bags so that we couldn't step on their floors. I wondered if it were not to save our shoes from the filth on their floors for we often needed a shoeshine after we came out.

We had friends at the American University in Cairo and at the Y.M.C.A, and from them we learned that the Y.M.C.A and a woman's club had been formed in the city about three years ago and membership was growing fast as women see their way out of the maze in which they are born. We had dinner with these friends who were all ministers except for the accountant who originated from Urbana, IL.

On our way to the airport, the cab driver was careful to point out to us three lovely palatial homes which are the gifts of King Farouck to his present mother-in-law. At the airport, we saw Samia Gamil, an Egyptian movie star and one of the King's favorite dancers, waiting for the Texas millionaire, Sheppard King to arrive. He did so while we were still there. They since have been married according to the papers.

Editor's note: They left Cairo on Sunday, October 7 for Kolundia Airport in the Jordanian controlled, divided city of Jerusalem and Hotel American Colony. They stayed in Jerusalem, both the Jordanian and Israeli-held sides, until Friday, October 19. It had been just a few years since the war between the Israelis and Arab countries in 1947.

October 7, 1951

Metropolitan Hotel in Cairo, Egypt (ed. note: written on this stationery, but mailed from Jerusalem)

Dear Folks and Kiddies,

We are now in Jerusalem. Our plane did not fly yesterday as it was scheduled to do. The visibility was too poor, so we stayed overnight in Cairo. It was very hot there, but much cooler here, maybe due to the rain last evening. We were eaten by mosquitoes during our stay in Cairo. You can never imagine how poor, yet how wealthy, and filthy it is. I couldn't believe it even when I saw it. Our hotel was one of the finest yet, we are covered with mosquito bites. They sprayed our room every day, but had no screens; none in Europe either, so flies and all came in at night for it was so hot we had to open windows. Needless to say we are glad we went to Cairo, but shall never want to go again as we don't like it.

Here in Jerusalem, the atmosphere is different. The houses and hotels are not like a big city and so far the people haven't had their hands out for money, money, money.

We shall tell you more of Jerusalem later. It seems impossible that we're here where Jesus lived and we should like to stay a long, long time to get the feel and the atmosphere of the country and the people.

Tell the children we wish they could be here with us. We can hear the school children from our window at the American Colony.

We went to church at the Scottish Presbyterian Church yesterday. Mostly the American University people attend. Love, pray for us and our safe return. Walt and Emma

Jordan and Holy Sites by Emma

After visiting Egypt, we flew from Cairo to Jordan near Jerusalem. The flight to Jordon was on a British Army plane with four seats. In route we went over the wilderness in which Moses and the children of Israel wandered for 40 years. Now I can understand why it took them 40 years to find their way out. It was sandy, rocky mountains. Where one ended another started, with no water to be seen between the Suez Canal and the Dead Sea, which is one-quarter minerals and utterly impossible to drink for I tasted it.

Jordon was another adventure with the antiquities and places surrounding Jesus' life. The Hashemite Kingdom of Jordan and the state of Israel were formed out of the country of Palestine. A north and south line, set up by the United Nations, divides the country and extends through the city of Jerusalem itself. In a perpetual state of war, the military police requested we show our passports. There were bitter feelings between the two countries.

Our cab driver guided us around Jordan to see the holy relics and towns there that were under Jordanian rule at the time. He was an Arab-Christian who had been "chased" from his home in Jerusalem by the Israelis during the 1947 war.

Europe and the Holy Land
By Walter, Emma, & Others

In Jerusalem, old on the Jordan side, we saw the first wire window screens that we had seen since we left New York. In this country, we reached the climax of our trip abroad for our aim was the Holy Land and practically all of it was on the Jordan side of the "line" (ed. note: today this part of Jordan is controlled by Israel, commonly referred to as the west bank).

In Jordan, women still balanced earthen jugs on their heads. They wash their clothes on stones at the springs, which were in existence from Biblical times. Here they got their drinking water, also. Clothes of the Palestinian refugee women were made of heavy material like blue denim, upon which they embroidered for years. Each village had its own embroidered design. If they had another dress, it probably was of linen, shantung, or silk with all of this elaborate hand work on it. Their headdress was made up of a cap often with dowry sewed on it. Over this they place a scarf -- some elaborate, some plain. The western dress was taking the place of this native costume, especially among those who were educated by the Christian church.

The men wore a robe like a dress with a flowing headdress or turban held in place with a black braided band. The children of the Palestinian refugees were professional beggars. They asked for "Baccache" (ed. note: we found no translation for this word). It broke our hearts to turn them down. The beasts of burden in this country were camels and donkeys. Many of the natives leave early in the day to pick up thistle or anything they could find for a fire.

The World Council of Churches first started giving food to these people before the U.N. saw the need and took over. It was poverty such as we have never seen and doesn't compare to our food problems; it is so much greater that it was almost unimaginable. If we could find ways to employ the people, all would be better.

As in most European countries, the average child goes only to the fifth or sixth grade and often then there aren't schools enough to go around, so shall we say the privileged few get the three "R's" -- then it is what we term "the old world" type of teaching where the child was taught to obey even though rebellion springs up inside them and they are taught what the teacher thinks they should know, not taught to think for themselves or given any initiative to do for themselves.

Agriculturally, Jordan was a wasteland. To me, it was barren desert, yet they did grow crops of bananas, oranges, lemons, grapes, beans, and always the fig and olive especially where they used irrigation. We saw one aqueduct in Jericho which had come over hills and mountains for many miles. Some of the olive trees must be a thousand years old. Some of the trunks were split into two or three parts, yet they lived and bore fruit.

Our first trip was to Samaria where we saw uncovered ruins of the old Ivory Palace of Ahab and Jezebel. Nearby were an old Roman fortress and a temple to Cesar Augusta. We saw three different kinds of walls; Greek, Roman, and Jewish.

We visited the home of the Samaritan High Priest. He, his brother and their wives, their children and their wives, and their grandchildren and their wives all lived under one roof. This High Priest was supposed to be a direct descendent of Aaron, Moses' brother. They showed us their small temple at the base of Mt. Garrison and an old, old scroll of the first four books of the Old Testament. These four books are all that the Samaritans feel are Holy.

Here we saw our first whitened sepultures, or burial places, then we saw what Jesus meant when he talked about being whitewashed on the outside and rotten on the inside.

On our way to Jericho and the Dead Sea, we stopped at Bethany to visit the home of Mary and Martha, which were dug from a stone cave. Then we went down underneath the ground to see the tomb of Lazarus. Nearby was the excavated site of three churches built one on top of the other, starting at the bottom with a Crusader's church with beautiful mosaic floor still there.

Another day we went to Hebron and stopped at the well where Abraham had his vision. At Hebron, we saw and entered the mosque that Herod built for the Jews over the Tombs of Abraham, Isaac, Jacob, Sarah, and Rebekah.

On the way to Bethlehem, we stopped at Phillip's fountain where

Phillip baptized the Ethiopian Eunuch. Here we saw women filling goatskins with water and loading them on donkeys.

In Bethlehem we saw Rachel's tomb. We went to the church that covers the cave where Jesus was claimed to have been born. Here one has to stoop to enter as though to bow before the manger. We also visited an orphanage and an insane institution. An old Roman aqueduct is partly there, built by Pilate with funds from the Temple. On this aqueduct we found waterproof plaster. This brought to mind how far the Romans had advanced to have decayed so much since. Bethlehem, which had been a city of 10,000 before all of this trouble started, was then a city of 70,000. Imagine the problems involved. The Palestinian refugee problem was terrific in the entire city as the water supply was so scarce in this country that all have to settle near water.

We spent one afternoon seeing the museum with architectural relics starting at the old stone age of man. In Jerusalem, the temple area was still remaining. Two mosques cover the spot where Solomon's temple had most probably stood. Here also town meetings had been held. From this area we could see where the Golden Gate to the old city was; from here we could also see the valleys of Kidron and Gehenna. We entered Sheep Gate, walked down the path Jesus was supposed to have gone to Calvary. This led through a present-day

Emma in Jordan, 1951

market place. The market was a crowded street where wares of all description were sold out of doors, food in one and jewelry in another.

We entered underground what was once part of King Herod's Court and trod on the old cobblestones. Now it is a nice Roman Catholic Church. At the end of the Dolorosa, "Way of the Cross" or "Way of Grief," is Calvary, which was also now a Roman Catholic Church. Nearby was a mosque on ground from which Jesus was supposed to have ascended into heaven.

Just outside of Damascus Gate we found a hill covered with a

Moslem Cemetery, called Gordon's Calvary. Just below were the remains of a rich man's garden where a cave tomb may be seen. This was kept by the Church of England.

Just out of the city was the Mount of Olives. We rode up one evening at dusk on the old Roman road which was only wide enough for one car to pass. It drove around the edge of the mount until we came to Bethphage, which was the place where Jesus sent his disciples to find a white donkey for his journey down to Jerusalem on Palm Sunday. The next day we went up there again and Mr. Smith (ed. note: not sure if this was Walter or another Mr. Smith) got out and walked down where we met him at the foot of the mount near the Garden of Gethsemane, which was filled with lovely flowers, old olive trees, and a Church of all nations.

The skies in the near east are clear as there was little rainfall, seven inches the previous year. The stars seem near. The evening star was so bright, I was sure it must be the Eastern Star that the wise men saw. A couple of American girls we met thought it was light from an airplane.

When it was time to cross into Israeli-held Jerusalem, our Arab cab driver took us to the barbed wire fence and gate dividing the city.

Israel by Emma

In Israel live Jewish people who at one time lived all over Palestine. Refugees from Europe, Asia, and America had established residence there. They told us that 1,000 people each day entered into this new country. These people were working hard at the job of getting the soil into shape to produce food and to teach the new comers a trade if they knew not one. The economy in Israel was poor as it was a new country then.

To enter the Israeli-held side of Jerusalem, we crossed through a gate guarded by solders. The city of Jerusalem was cut through the middle with barbed wire fences. We had to walk through the gate with our luggage and get a taxi on the Israeli side. The cab took us to the

Y.M.C.A where we had a poor lunch. We met a boy who was attending school on a Rotary scholarship.

The Y.M.C.A. was across the street from the King David Hotel. It was almost a boundary. The last message in the War of 1947 between the Jews and Arabs was to "lower your fire, you're hitting the Y.M.C.A." Both sides had a profound respect for it. The Y.M.C.A. itself was one of the most beautiful in the world.

From there we went on to Tel Aviv, the capital of Israel. It was a Saturday and nothing was open at all because of the Jewish holy day. We had a hard time finding a hotel, motel, or tourist room until Walter took off his Christian lapel pin of a cross.

Tel Aviv, which was very much in the news then, was on the Mediterranean seacoast and was one of the most modern cities in the world. It was near the old harbor town of Joppa. It was a nice experience. Israel was very isolated at the time.

The Israelis had lots of farms and used modern technology, so their country looks so much better than that of Jordan. They lived on cooperative farms called a kibbutz. Everyone had a job, even mothers. The children were cared for by

Emma & Walter in Israel, 1951

nurses, teachers, and supervisors, in a little world of their own. The parents came on certain days to visit and play with their children.

In a newspaper or magazine, we read about a kibbutz in Israel. They had written in the article, "If anyone comes over to Israel they can stay at our house." We had corresponded with Israelis living in a kibbutz (ed. note: Mr. and Mrs. Leon Shamir.) They invited us to spend a few days with them on their small farm. We took overalls and blue work shirts for them that they had requested. In those days, everything was scarce in Israel.

We stayed with friends in one of the kibbutz for two days. In this cooperative, each couple started with two rooms and worked to gain larger homes, land, and cattle. The crops were owned by all the people in the cooperative. The people owned nothing but their labor. All food was cooked and shared in one place. The homes and clothing were what the cooperative committee bought. Everyone works and loves for the community's good.

Military service was required of both boys and girls at the age of 18. Part of the time in service was spent in military training and part in land development, where the youth were taught to care for the land. Many of them liked it so well that when they married they settle on a farm. They told us that the boys and girls who grow up in the cooperative communities go to service much easier than the ones who live in their own homes, get less homesick, and adjust to living with others much easier for they are used to it.

In Israel, we met a cab driver for American Express Travel Services, a Baptist minister, Y.M.C.A instructor and his wife, and a minister of the Scottish Presbyterian Church.

October 16, 1951
Israel

Dear Folks,

Well, here we are in Israel. We had no difficulty crossing the divide in Jerusalem from Jordon to Israel, but there was an awful lot of red tape, police permits, visa customs, etc. etc. They looked through our bags when we left the Jordon side and again when we entered the Israeli side. How they dislike and distrust each other. How Christ must weep over Jerusalem today.

We went to the Scottish Presbyterian Church in Jerusalem, then to the Y.M.C.A. for dinner. There isn't much food here in Israel and so expensive. We shall be glad to get home to lunch meat, wieners, have fried chicken, beans and cornbread, lettuce, and water. It will not be so long now until we shall be there.

Today is a Jewish holiday and very few things are open, so we are resting. Tonight we can find out about our passage

*to Athens, then go up to Tiberius and Galilee knowing when
we must be back here.*

The Holy Land was a highlight (<u>ed. note</u>: many parts
of the Holy Land were under Jordanian control in 1951
before the Arab-Israeli wars of the 1960s and 1970s.)
*Oh, how we enjoyed every minute of it. We had an Arab-
Christian guide and he made the Bible live for us.*

*Give our love to all. We are very weary and very homesick.
Home will look very good to us when we get there. Glad to
hear fine reports on the children. It makes us feel good to know
they are doing well.*

*We have had only a few stomach upsets from the food
and mostly water. We have kept moving along though to see
all. The doctor gave us medicine before we left and it cleared
us right up.*

*If your table cloth should arrive before us, you should not
have to pay duty on it as we shall declare it when we re-enter
the U.S. probably early November. We can declare $500
worth each and we haven't bought anywhere near that amount
between us.*

*This girl from Israel is sending coins to Bud, stamps to
Dave, and a birthday gift to Kaye. It should be there any day.*

*I left a birthday card for Bud either in upper left-hand
drawer of chest in bedroom or bottom drawer of downstairs desk.
Walt and Emma*

<u>Editor's note</u>: On or before Friday, October 19, they arrived in Athens
and stayed at Hotel Grand Bretagne.

Greece by Emma

From Israel we flew to Athens, Greece. All of Greece was hit hard
by the War (<u>ed. note</u>: probably their civil war after WW II.) There
were very few tourists. Greek homes had crosses of the Greek Orthodox
Church on them. The people were backward, but very friendly. The

children marched to school with the teacher as their leader and wore uniforms. I wondered about recess and their classes.

We truly loved the Acropolis, all the buildings and ruins. The guards stood in wooden box shelters in uniform. They never moved or smiled and we tried to make them.

We bought bus tickets to old Corinth. We could speak no Greek and they no English. The tickets showed where we were going. At Corinth was a restaurant. Since we could not read the menu, they took us to the kitchen to pick out our food. When we finished, we held Greek coins in our hands and they picked out the amount for our meals. We trusted them completely.

October 20, 1951

Athens, Greece (<u>ed. note</u>: written on stationery from British European Airways)

Dear Folks and Children,

We stayed in Athens two days less than we had planned for we could see all we needed to in that length of time -- and all was quite expensive there -- besides we are getting so homesick that any distance closer seems better to us, I guess.

We are in the air now toward Rome. We go down to Naples by train to the Methodist orphanage there, Casa Materna (<u>ed. note</u>: they received at least four postcards from people at this orphanage over the next few years.)

We saw the Bethlehem orphanage and gave them our money. They are doing wonderful work there. The manager is very nice.

We've had a most wonderful trip and are now very ready to return home. We do so hope our pictures turn out well.

Enclosed is a sticker for the children's suitcase. Love all of them for us. Will you have time to write us a letter to New York by November 5-6? Here is the address -- airmail will take 2-3 days from Olney c/o American Express, 65 Broadway, New York, N.Y.

We shall telegram when we arrive in N.Y. and know how and when we shall get home. If we have money enough we may fly so we can spend a few days in N.Y. We didn't get to see it at all and we'd like to compare it to the other big cities we've seen here.

If we fly, I hope the children can be along to meet us for it is a great experience to see big planes coming and going and how they would love it. We shall see and you use your own judgement. Let you know our plans as soon as we know them. Love and prayers, Walt and Emma

Italy Again by Emma

While in Naples, Italy we visited an American orphanage created after World War I at a villa on the Mediterranean Sea that was given to them by the church. We knew about this orphanage, Casa Materna or "motherly house," and they invited us to stay with them. The Methodists had given them some money. It was on the Mediterranean and we stayed at least a week with them. We ate all our meals with them and left them with a nice donation.

A Methodist pastor, Dr. Riccardo Santi, and his wife took in children from the streets in 1905, and later during WWII, who were orphans and often lived in caves. He took them into his home. There were more and more. Later, one of his parishioners gave him his beautiful estate, home and land behind rock walls, which was on the Mediterranean Sea. They made an orphanage of it. It is beautiful property.

The girls were taught housekeeping and gardening. The boys were taught to make furniture and had made all of it for the dormitories. The Methodist church helped to keep it running. The estate was 45 years old with 200 children -- 165 more were in school there. Dr. Santi's sons were a lawyer, doctor, and a daughter taught kindergarten there. Dr. Santi still goes to slums and caves to minister to the poor.

<u>Editor's note</u>: The top left-hand corner of the following letter from Walter and Emma to their children was torn off, which cut off some of the writing on the back page. In addition, the ink "bled" on both sides, making it difficult to decipher either side of the letter. Ellipses are used to show where words are not legible. The stamps on the envelope were pictures of the rocks of Gibraltar. They must have bought the stamps in Rome.

October 25, 1951

> *Thought you might enjoy a letter with the pictures of the rocks on it and mailed from Gibraltar. We shall get there tonight at midnight. We are sorry for we wish it were day so we could see what it looks like. We stop there for an hour.*
>
> *The Mediterranean was rough yesterday as everyone, including me but not your daddy, was sick. Hardly anyone ate noon lunch. Today it is better and all are up and going. We have had fairly good meals onboard ship.*
>
> *We are so very anxious to get back home to work. It has been a fine vacation, but ... too long. Hope all is going well and Grandma is not worn out. Be good boys and girls.*
>
> *There are 700 tourists ... ship and only 150 second ... 150 first class. It is ... many for the space ... there is lots of confusion and ... space outside our cabin to relax. We are very thankful we have a cabin to ourselves. 200 of the tourist class are Italian boys going to Canada to work for the government. Practically all on ship speak Italian, a few English. Most are people who have come to Italy from America to visit relatives. Very few are tourists.*
>
> *We are wondering how much you children have grown and how much you have learned at school and who your new playmates are. Love and kisses to everyone and we shall see you about November 8 or 9 or 10. Love, mother and dad*

October 25, 1951
> *Telegramma from Napoli, Italia to Walter and Emma Smith via the S.S. Saturnia, which is bound for New York*
>> *Hope you have a pleasant trip home. Thanks again for the film. Bon voyage. Betty and Charlie Ozias*

November 5, 1951, 3:58 p.m.
> *Western Union Telegram to Mrs. Ross Smith at 319 South Fair in Olney, Illinois*
>> *Arriving via Pennsylvania Railroad, Effingham at noon, November sixth. Meet us. Walter*

Conclusion by Emma

As for the ship ride home, I was seasick on the way as I was carrying another child, John "Mark" Smith, who was born in April 1952 in the Olney Hospital after we returned home.

We're thankful that we were born and live in America with clean water, clean grocery stores, education for all, and city services of electricity and garbage collection, etc. Also, we have freedom of religion. We can be thankful for this by being tolerant of other's way of living, worshiping, and thinking. Women are treated better here than in any other country in the world. However, women are essentially alike all over the world for they love their children, love their home, and love their husbands.

Editor's note: As I was wondering how safe it was for a young couple to travel in Europe and the Holy Lands in the 1950s, I asked someone who travelled often. Here is his reply of his experience.

The only place I got "rolled" was when I was in Paris. I was young. I went to a museum, I was by myself. I was coming out and there was a courtyard. Some "gypsy kids" came along and one of them said he wanted some money. There were about fifteen of them. They were only 10 or 12 years old. They wouldn't leave me alone. I told them to "get out of here," and one on the other side got my bag. They took my wallet, passport, credit cards, checks, everything. There I was without anything.

Along came a Frenchman on a motorcycle and he let me ride with him to a nearby police station. The police said that there wasn't anything they could do about it because the kids were minors. The Frenchman then took me to the Embassy on his motorcycle. I had a money belt and in it I had a list of every traveler's check by number. I gave them the numbers right there and they gave me replacement checks. I showed them a photocopy of my passport. They made a new one right there. The Embassy even called all of my credit card companies and cancelled them all. That was scary. I was alone with no money or friends with me.

Flora by Emma

By the time Mark was six months old, Walter was appointed Superintendent of the Olney District and the family all too soon moved from Olney to Flora in 1952 to spend the next six years. At only 37 years old, Walter was the youngest Superintendent in the country at that time.

I remember moving to Flora and living at the edge of town. We had only the one car. Walter used it for work most of the time. The house was too small for us, it had no shade, one window air conditioner, but it did have a dishwasher. I was thankful for that.

The boys, three of them, had a big room, Walter and I had the second bedroom, so we converted the furnace room for Kaye who had a youth bed so it was acceptable for the space. We were not comfortable there as we had come from a large house with four bedrooms, one of which we used as a playroom for the children; there were three in those days and a baby, Mark. It also had a front and a back staircase, which was convenient.

I remember getting so aggravated that the children didn't keep their rooms neat. They were to make their beds or at least pull them together and at least once each year rid them of unwanted items. I think it must have rubbed off on me for now I'm having trouble ridding myself of unwanted and unneeded "things." Now they can get aggravated with me.

Cooking was another challenge. We had no quick way to fix meals. Everything had to be peeled, skinned, or shucked. I seldom had to pick them from the garden as the kids helped. At least I always had a gas or electric stove and a refrigerator.

During these six years, Walter was gone a great amount of time. He held quarterly conferences at each charge. He got to know his pastor's families and most of them had him for dinner on his visits. They appreciated his interest in them. One of his main goals was to put plumbing with indoor bathrooms in each parsonage. When his six years was up, he had accomplished this goal.

I had most of the care of the house and the children. We found the parsonage to which we were assigned was in a country school district.

Dave was in the fourth grade, Kaye in third, and Charlie in first grade. After that first year, the people in that area petitioned to consolidate into the Flora grade school and everyone was happier.

Debbie was born while we lived here. I often kept her up late so she could visit with her dad who usually left in the mornings before she was awake.

In Flora, we heard a loud "plop!" Charlie had fallen out of the top bunk bed. Mark was sleeping underneath, but the noise didn't wake him up.

When Debbie was eighteen months old, Walter went to Japan with the Lacour Mission group. Another pastor paid his way to Japan and for his keep. A Japanese student-interpreter stayed with him, ate with him, and worked with him while in Japan. It took some "getting used to" to learn the Japanese culture and live and eat like they did, so he could teach them Christianity.

Editor's note: The following are childhood memories of Flora by their children.

We lived on North 12th Street in Flora. Milk was delivered to us each morning. A sewer system was installed behind our house. The house had a very hot flat roof garage. The people who lived behind us had a field with horses.

Dad bought a small farm while in Flora. He bought a three-wheel tractor for it.

We went to a one room school in the country. It was first through eighth with two teachers. We rode the bus to school and walked home afterwards.

We have random memories of chickens with no heads trying to fly and many cases of hominy.

We remember camping at Charlie Brown State Park after dad and mom bought a fourteen-foot camper. It slept three, but five of us slept in it and two in a pup tent outside. Dad and mom had the master bed, Kaye used the dinette that made into a bed, Mark slept on the floor and the baby, Deb slept at the foot of her parents.

<u>Editor's note</u>: In 1957 while living in Flora, Walter participated in a missionary trip to Japan. Most of the following are letters written by Walter while he was participating in the Lacour Mission of Japan. The missionaries converted Japanese people to Christianity. Some of the letters below were addressed to his church supporters. No letters from the U.S. addressed to Walter were found among his belongings. His letters are in *italics*. We begin with a newspaper announcement of Walter's missionary trip.

Missionaries in Japan, 1957

Clay County Advocate-Press

FLORA, 1957 -- Dr. Walter A. Smith, district superintendent of the Olney District of the Methodist Church, left last Sunday and is now working in Japan. Dr. Smith was sent by the Methodist Board of Missions to work on the Lacour Mission, which is sponsored by the United Church of Christ of Japan.

A similar mission has been conducted for the past three summers with work done in 27 unchurched areas. This year there are thirty (people) on the mission from the United States -- 24 ministers and six wives. Of this group, 13 are Methodists, five are Presbyterian, three Disciples of Christ, two Evangelical and Reformed, and one Evangelical United Brethren. Each person is assigned a particular center in which to work.

The workers (ed. note: the missionaries) each have an interpreter to aid in their work. This person is usually one of the Seminary students. There is also a Japanese pastor and wife to assist in the program.

Many villages in Japan have Christians but no organized church. This is part of the purpose of the mission and the other is to reach others as new followers for Christ in the Christian way.

The activities will be many and varied including: open air preaching, showing of filmstrips such as those of the life of Christ, personal counseling of seekers (of Christ), youth meetings, children's Bible story hour, training of Sunday School teachers, choir work as the Japanese people delight in song, Bible Study groups for adults, recreation such as picnics and the fascinating American baseball, and all phases of worship. As Dr. Smith states, "We all will be busy every minute of our waking hours."

There are twenty-seven centers of work and four of them are self-supporting. It is hoped that the others may follow the same pattern just as soon as possible and as a result of the mission.

Missionary Letters from the Far East by Walter

July 2, 1957
Dear Sweethearts:

Well, I have just had a wonderful night's sleep on the beautiful island of Hawaii. We have a spacious room on the beach. We can see the blue Pacific Ocean. This is truly an enchanting place. Hope you can see it sometime.

We arrived in San Francisco yesterday at around 6 and left at 10 a.m. They have a beautiful airport there. It is all new and nice. Just as I was getting on the plane the checker told me they had lost my bag. United Airlines had not delivered it. "Grand way to start the trip," I thought. The Pam-Am man said they would do their best to find it and it would catch up with me. I worried some about it anyway. When we pulled in here they were paging me. My bag was here. I was relieved.

Last night my roommate and I took a long walk around the city here. By the way, he is Harold Dorsey of Prestonburg, KY. What a tourist paradise with beautiful hotels and shops. There was a definite flavor of the "old World" and the "Islands of Pacific."

"Conked Out" Engine, 1957

Mother, you would have been in your glory and the styles! Wow!

We are a long way from home -- about 4,700 air miles. It has taken 16 flying hours. That figures 300 miles per hour, almost exactly. The trip over the ocean was very smooth. We travelled at 305 miles per hour all the way until one motor "conked out" -- then only 250 mi. per hour.

Everyone was a little worried with only 3 engines pulling us, but the purser (ed. note: an officer on a ship) assured us that they could make it fine on just two engines.

We have orientation here at the Methodist Church after a while, so must close and get ready. Pray for us every day. Love to all. Dave, you help mother with the kids and the yard. Kaye, you take good care of Debby. Buddy and Mark, you stay close to home so mother won't worry about you. Walter

July 5, 1957
Dear Emma and all:

Well, we have been in Tokyo about a day. It is some city; large, dirty, and filled with all kinds of people. We are situated in the Imperial Hotel. It is a lovely place. We have a nice air-conditioned room. I am still rooming with Harold Dorsey from Prestonburg, KY.

How are all of you? Did Debbie get over her cold? Did she resent you going to Chicago? Did Buddy and Mark say anything more about our leaving? How did Dave and Kaye like the trip to Chicago?

We do not have our assignments yet. Will get them Saturday afternoon and I will write you again then. We have had very interesting orientation talks. One of the men said that we would crowd all of the joys and sorrows of a missionary's life into two months.

We have Saturday, tomorrow off and I am going with a small group to Nikko. This is one of the real beauty spots of Japan. So you see, though we have had such a busy schedule, I have not had time to shop any yet. We do get to mix in some pleasure with our business.

Will write more soon. I have not heard from you yet. Love to all, Walter

Saturday, July 6
Dear Mother and all:

I wrote a letter last night and carried it around in my pocket all day today trying to find stamps. I hope to find some and send it on to you anyhow.

We went to Nikko today. It was a very wonderful experience. This is a great center of Buddhist worship. We saw a number of Shrines there and went into one Buddhist sanctuary.

Nikko is also a resort city with a lovely lake 4000 feet above sea level and a beautiful water fall. There were just four out of our group who went. A little Japanese girl, a P.K. (ed. note: a preacher's kid) *acted as our guide and interpreter. Her name, Kaiko, means grace and she is a senior in college. With such a small group we had a very interesting time.*

We got home, here at the Imperial Hotel at 8:30 p.m. and I found that my assignment for the summer is at a small town, Oji. Oji is between Nara and Osaka. You will find these cities, also Fuse, on your map. Oji is near them. I will write more about the place just as soon as I learn more.

We are to have a private conference with the Lacours just as soon as we can to give us detailed information on our centers (ed. note: "centers" were the towns where the missionaries were stationed that summer.) *The Lacours are very fine. They have prepared for this mission nicely. Our whole team is very congenial. I am praying for a great mission this summer. Japan needs it, our Japanese preachers want it, and it will help all of us American ministers, too.*

By the way, I have not had the slightest sickness yet. Pray for us, Walter A. Smith

July 8, 1957 -- 7 p.m.
Dear Kuga's: (ed. note: probably referring to a term used in Japan to refer to things one owns)

Is Debbie learning to talk anymore? We are having a great time, but I wish that I could see you. We had another day of orientation and were assigned to our centers. We will be leaving Tokyo on Wednesday. I think I told you that I am to be stationed at Oji near Nara. My address will be: Kakimoto Ryokan, Shinkisan-jo, Nara-Ken, Japan. My interpreter is a college student named Yoshiaki Kikuchi. I will call him Kē Kū chē-san. My pastor is Rev. Nakashima. The "a" is pronounced as in Amen and the "i" is pronounced as a long ē.

I have finally had a little time to shop today. I bought two filters for my camera that will let the lens door close and a tripod. The tripod cost $6.00 and the filters $1.25 each.

There is wonderful silk pongee and shantung at $1.67 per yard (ed. note: pongee is a soft and typically unbleached type of plain-woven Chinese fabric, originally made from threads of raw silk and now other fibers also such as cotton. Shantung is a fabric that is commonly made with silk, which comes from the cocoon of the silkworm.) *Which would you rather have, pongee or shantung? They also have white blouse material. The raw silk costs about $1.00 per yard. It is in beautiful plaids for shirts for Kaye. They also have silk suiting at $1.67 per yd. Would you like some of these?*

Concerning the china, the Noritake costs from $41 to $50 in service for 12 persons and about $25 for shipping. This is high enough, but here is the joke. Just to ship one set costs the same as two or three. The shipping on 2 sets and 3 or 4 tea sets would be about $20.00. Aiko, Wanda's interpreter, is going to try to get it cheaper through a friend. It is very beautiful stuff. They say it is better than the kind they export.

The pearls are very nice. The cheapest necklaces are about $8.50 and they go as high as you please. The ear-rings are $5.00 up. The crystal necklaces are also lovely. They are from $8.00 up. Ear-rings are lovely, too. I have found several beautiful vases. They range from $8.00 to $12.00 each. This seems very expensive.

Don't bother about Hodson's letter. And, there is no flu scare here. By the way the Imperial Hotel is a very lovely place. The Inn where I am going is very nice I am told. Let us hope so.

I have received three letters, two from you and one from Ernie. In my next letter I will tell you about my center and my *interpreter. Dr. Lacour is going with us out to Kobe to introduce us to our workers and supervising ministers there. Mine is a rather expensive place to live. It will cost me about $40 beside my expenses here in Tokyo now and at the end of the mission. Glad Dr. Lacour has the $100 deposit for me.*

Sorry David's team is not doing so well. I hear by the paper that the Cardinals are back in first place. We get an English newspaper every day.

Tell Buddy and Mark that I miss them as well as you all. Tell Kaye to work hard on her dress for I want her to get a blue ribbon.

Explain about the china to the Martins'. The total cost will be between $50 and $60. You can do about as well from Montgomery Ward I fear. However, you all be the judge. My love and prayers are for you. Sincerely with love, Walter

July 10, 1957
Dear Folks:

Yesterday, we were on the train all day coming from Tokyo to Kobe. We have a conference here today with all of our pastors and interpreters then go out to our centers.

My center is Oji. It is a little town of 8,500 people. That is considered a very small country village. We have a pastor and wife who are very young. He has just graduated from Theological School. He speaks English very "frequently" as my interpreter said. He meant "fluently." We are going to have a good time, I am sure. My interpreter is just fair, but we will get along.

I am now at the Y.M.C.A in Kobe. We are spending two nights here before going to our centers. It is not deluxe like the Imperial Hotel in Tokyo, but it is comfortable. I am sitting on my bed writing on my lap. The bed is an iron bed, single. In the room there is a closet, lavatory, small table, and chair.

The room is about 8' by 10'. The floor has no varnish. The Japanese do not bother to paint or varnish their houses much. Therefore, they look old after two or three years.

Last night we had a lovely experience. After riding on the train all day, we were hurried here to the Y.M.C.A to leave our bags and on to a missionary's home for supper. It was a delightful evening sitting around small tables in their home and talking about Japanese customs and our work this summer. The Lacours have certainly tried to prepare us for our work.

Oji was opened as a church two summers ago. The first year they got 2 baptized Christians. Last year they added 4 more. We now have 6 members. However, there are 12 or 14 "seekers." We hope to double the membership this summer. Pray for us.

I will write you about my Inn just as soon as I get there.

I gave my new address on the last letter. That may be changed. I will let you know promptly what it is. Are all of the children well? Write me the news. Give my love to all. Sincerely with love, Walter

July 15, 1957
Oji, Japan

Dearest:

Well, I am at last situated in my room for the summer. When I came to Oji last Friday, they put me in an Inn about 20 minutes ride from here. Lacour protested because I was so inaccessible to the people. They could not spend the money to come to see me. It cost 140 yen to go. So the pastor found my interpreter, Kikuchi, and me adjourning rooms in the apartment house. My room is about 9' by 12' and Kikuchi-san's is smaller. We have it fixed up quite Western with an army bed, a desk, and a chair. In one end are closets and a nice wash basin. This is my first day here. I like it much better than the Inn.

We had real service at the Inn. There were two or three maids in charge of our comfort. All of our meals were served in our room and the food was fair.

We now plan to have a simple breakfast of rolls and milk. The milk is delivered daily and we can plan ahead for rolls. Japanese pastries are quite good. At noon we will go to a "crummy" restaurant where the food will be so-so. At night we will have a nice meal delivered to our rooms. Tonight we had a wonderful hamburger steak. Japanese vegetables are unbelievably atrocious. The rice dishes are very good. We will make out all right, I am sure. I have my chlorine tablets. Am I glad! The water here is from a well. With these open sewers that means beware. This afternoon I found a shop which handles orange, lemon, grape, and pineapple syrups. I bought a bottle. That makes my chlorine water taste very good. My great fear is that I shall gain weight instead of losing.

We had wonderful services our first Sunday out here. There were 43 children and 7 adults in the morning Sunday school. There were 18 adults at worship service. I wish you could have heard these children sing. There is a fine young Superintendent about 20 years of age. The pastor plays the portable organ and they "go to town." The pastor and his wife, Mr. and Mrs.

Walter in Oji, Japan, 1957

Nakashima -- pronounced Nä Kä shēē mä, are grand with the children in the classes, too.

About the pastor, he graduated from seminary in March and came to Oji in April of this year. He is getting off to a fine start. They are in their twenties and the people seem to love them.

Today, they are gone to Osaka to see the doctor. Mrs. Nakashima is not well. The pastor thinks she may have appendicitis, but I don't. She has a familiar nausea. They have been married about two years. They are a very attractive couple.

My space is about exhausted. I will report more at a later time. Pray for our church daily. We have only 6 members. This must be doubled this summer. My love to you all, Walter

P.S. My address is: Takaraso Apartments, Jimmankasa-Macji, Ikaruga-cho, Ikoma-san, Nara-Ken, Japan.

July 16, 1957
Oji, Japan

Dear Friends of the Olney District:

I am writing you from the town of Oji, pronounced Oh Gee, in the heart of Japan. First, I send my thanks to all who helped to make this mission possible. It is truly a great work. It would be wonderful if all of you could have this experience of pioneering for Christ in a strange land.

Let me describe the field. Oji is a town of about 10,000 people. It is a farm trading center and the largest industry is the making of stockings. It is located just thirty minutes by express train northeast of Osaka, and not far from Kyoto, the old capital of Japan. It is in the very center of Buddhist and Shinto worship. From the window of the Inn where I stayed the first few nights, I could see a beautiful large temple surrounded by innumerable shrines. To win converts for Christ here is most difficult.

In 1956 there was an attempt to start a church here. A few meetings have been held in the meantime and we are trying some more now. Our church is a little room downtown that is about fifteen by twenty-five feet. It is clean with a straw mat floor and a pulpit. There are no pews. The people sit on the floor around low tables about 15 inches high.

Last Sunday we had forty-three children in Sunday school and six or seven adults. I wish that you could hear these children sing. The Superintendent is a college student, a fine young man. He led the singing, responses and prayers, while our pastor played the portable table organ. It was great! The pastor, his wife and the Superintendent divided the children into three classes.

At the worship service we had eighteen adults and I had the second experience of speaking through an interpreter. The people listened very intently. At the evening service, Dr. Lacour visited our town and we had a great outdoor mass meeting. Dr. Lacour preached a good sermon and twenty-four people signed interest cards. These are some of our "prospects." Two movies were shown, one for the children, "The Prodigal Son," and one for the adults, "Dust and Destiny." About 400 people attended this service. The purpose of this meeting was two-fold: to secure the names of interested people and to introduce me to the town to describe our mission.

There is great need for a Christian witness. In a town of about 10,000 there is no other church but our effort. The pastor and I feel very deeply both about the opportunity and about our inadequacy. Please pray that we will be good witnesses for Christ here. You cannot imagine the need. I appreciate your friendship very much, and solicit your prayers. Please pray for us by name.

There are many things besides the strange culture to discourage us. All night long we fight mosquitoes and bugs, and day and night there are atrocious smells. In the very best Inn, I ate and slept Japanese style on the floor. And the food! Oh, how I appreciate our western homes and good sanitation. However, I am neither discouraged nor greatly homesick. Some of us here live in the faith that your prayers ascend daily and that sustains us.

The harvest truly is ready and God is the Lord of that harvest. Sincerely yours, Walter A. Smith

P.S. Please note my address given on page one.

Friday, July 17, 1957
9 a.m. here, 7 p.m. yesterday at home

Dear Folks:

Evidently by now you have forgotten that you have a dad. It has been ten days today since I heard from you. Do you not know that "the Christian News" will forward my mail no matter where I am? Fortunately, since hearing from you, I have had three letters: one from Ernie, one from the Robinsons, and one from Brother Wilkerson. This helps.

Although we are relatively busy, the time passes slowly here. Still, I have only thirty-seven more days here at the Center, then back to Tokyo for three days, then around the world home. I have not heard from the Airlines about my stop-over in Calcutta. They are working on it for me; also hotel reservations. I have my visa for India. No others needed.

Last night we had our first Bible Class. Eleven young people joined the pastor, my interpreter and me for the study. The young people here are very much interested in English and in the Bible, especially the New Testament. We are using as a text in addition to the New Testament, a little Y.M.C.A. book called "A Christian's Faith." It takes up various teachings of Jesus and deals with them simply. Young people seem to enjoy it.

My interpreter is an interesting young man. He comes from a poor family, but they are sacrificing to send him to college. He is now in his second year and apparently doing well. He was telling me yesterday that once he went without food for three days. He said that it was a great experience. His parents usually sent money on a certain day, but this time they forgot. He had foolishly spent all of his money on the day before he was to receive his new allowance. He said "I don't believe that I could have stood it had I known it was going to be three days. I did without one meal at a time, thinking surely my money could come before the next day. You can always do without one meal if you think you will get the next one. It was a great experience in faith. On the third day I began to get weak and dizzy. My eyesight changed and the world looked strange. I noticed that everyone looked wonderful." He said it was also good for him because it cleaned out his stomach. I guess it was empty. He looks undernourished now. I have been trying to fatten him up. With rice, spaghetti, noodles, etc. at about 15 cents per dish, I can afford to feed him a lot of it.

They have stiff entrance exams here for college. He told me that 45 took exams on the day he did and only two passed them. Their colleges are so crowded that they will take only the most promising ones. Still it is a bad system. I asked him if he had a scholarship and he answered that he started to take the test, but found students from poorer families competing and decided not to try. That is the way it is. I will order a beef steak lunch and he will say that it costs too much for me, please order me noodles. It has rained every day since we came out to Oji and yesterday I opened my apartment window and saw a snake. I called Kikuchi to see it. He said, "Oh, this is Africa, and we live on the edge of the jungle." There is a weed and brush patch behind the apartments. The mosquitoes and bugs swarm in our rooms out of them every night. Glad I have my bug bombs. They have a sort of fuse that burns slowly all night, smoking and driving away the bugs. I spray and use one of those things, too. The smoke has a vile odor, but it is better by far than fighting mosquitoes.

By the way, we had to take Mrs. Nakashima, the pastor's wife, to the hospital. She has internal troubles. Her organs have slipped out of place. She will have to be there about a week then she can rest at home. The pastor is spending a lot of time going back and forth. This hinders the work some, but we are doing enough I think.

There is a wonderful opportunity here for a church. I sense a lot of interest on the part of young and old. If we can give them a good idea of Christianity, perhaps some will accept it and become loyal Christians. Continue to pray for us. Last Sunday Kikuchi prayed for lunch. Although he does not plan to enter the ministry, his major is economics, he said in his prayer, "Father I thank thee that I had a chance to Preach the Gospel this morning." He interpreted my sermon. "May we be able to win many Christians before the end of the summer." It is an inspiration to me to see the faith of these boys.

Well, you can tell by this letter that I am getting along well. I don't think that I have lost any of my spare tire yet. Please keep these letters, for I may want to refer to them later for my records. As Grandma says, "Hello David, Hello Kaye, Hello Buddy, Hello Mark, and Hello Debbie." Please give all of the Kids a big hug for me. My Love to you all, Walter

P.S. The pastor has loaned me his typewriter. It does not spell every well sometimes. Ha!

July 21, 1957, 10 p.m. Tokyo
7 a.m. Saturday Flora

Dear David, Kaye, Bud, Mark, Debbie, and Mother:

Today, I finally received two letters from you. I had not heard from you since July 8ᵗʰ. The two letters that came were the one from David, and the one in which you said were some enclosures. The letter had come unsealed and only had a one letter and the super Kodachrome film. I suggest that when you

*send enclosures that you use stronger envelopes. Did you receive
my letter with the sample illustrations of china enclosed?*

*Tell David that I have just heard a sports cast on the
pastor's radio upstairs. The Cardinals had beat Pittsburgh 9 to
4 but had dropped to third place since I had heard last, behind
Philadelphia and Milwaukee. I also read that Von McDaniel
had lost his first major league game.*

*We had fair services today. There were about 48 children
in Sunday school plus 7 adults. We had 15 in worship. There
were 9 at the youth meeting and 9 at evening service. With
only six members and all of them having to work so hard, this is
good. We have some non-Christians at every service. Perhaps
we can win some of them. Continue to pray for us.*

*Did I tell you that we had to take the pastor's wife to
the hospital? She has been there a week tomorrow, and is
improving only very slowly. Her blood count is about one-third
what it should be. This hinders our calling, because she is in
Osaka and Rev. Nakashima must go to see her every day. We
are probably doing enough anyway. The work here is slow.*

*I am glad to hear about Bud's haircut. Also, I am glad to
know David is helping with the yard and hedge. Debbie will
be talking a lot by the time I get home. Tell Mark that I want
to see if he can swim when I get home and Kaye to make a
blue ribbon on her dress.*

*Last Friday night we had a youth caravan from Osaka.
There were six young men led by an American missionary.
They held a service for children in the afternoon and a public
meeting at night. At the children's service they showed a film
on the creation of the world and gave an interesting puppet show
on the Good Samaritan. One of the men then told a story of a
courageous Japanese boy who gave his life to save many others
and made a fine application about Christ dying upon the cross
for us. I doubt if there were 5 children from Christian homes
there. This is a fine witness and I am sure deep impressions
are being made. At night the boys gave the story of how they*

became Christians. Only one of them came from a Christian home. They all gave a fine tribute to the American missionary. The American missionary preached a good sermon on "Ask and it will be given you, Seek, and you will find, Knock and it will be open unto you."

Today I preached on the subject, "God Needs You." They listened very intently. I am trying to get a tape recorder to record me preaching through the interpreter. I also want you to hear these children sing, pray, and study the bible together.

Did I describe the church to you? It is a little room about 15 feet by 25 feet. Everyone sits on the mat floor, except the preacher who stands behind a pulpit at the end of the room. The little tables are just about 15 inches high. There is a little portable organ. The services are very nice. I hope to have a recording of one of them for you to hear.

How is my garden coming? Are the tomatoes ripe yet? Are the new beans about ready to bloom? Who hoes the garden now? I am afraid of the answers to these questions. My poor garden may be sadly neglected. I wonder about the flowers, the Marigolds and Mums? We are having tomatoes every day here. They, and the beef steak, are about the two best things I eat. You would be surprised at the vegetables. The green beans and carrots are good but they are only cooked about 5 minutes or perhaps less. They taste raw.

Tonight we ate with Rev. Nakashima and his sister. His sister fixed a wonderful salad bowl and all of us over-ate. It had tomatoes, potatoes, ham, boiled eggs, cucumbers, lettuce, etc. mixed with a small portion of salad dressing. After curry rice, chicken rice, beef rice, white rice, and more rice, that salad tasted delicious. I still haven't lost my "spare tire."

I like the apartment here just fine. There are some handicaps, the restrooms with the open sewer, WOW! Sometimes I get a whiff of smells beyond description. I do not go to the public bath downtown. There are two nice public baths here in Oji, but I have not gotten the courage to go yet. There is a big wash basin in my room where I can get a nice "sponge bath." I also do a small washing every day. I have not worn my cotton shirts yet. The Dacron ones are so easy to keep clean.

By the way I have not received my box with the food stuff. I have heard that it was badly damaged and that the coffee was broken in shipment. I don't know about the rest of it. I received one package sent by Vernie. There is supposed to be another.

I suppose that I go over these same things every time. Is there anything about the town, pastor, interpreter, church, customs, etc. that you are curious about? I will try to give you as good a picture as I can.

Well, it is 11 p.m. I must close. My love to all. Give all of the kids a hug for me. Good night, Dad

P.S. Don't worry too much about my address. Letters addressed as shown on the return will reach me quickest, but the Christian News will forward promptly.

July 23, 1957 -- 10 p.m.
7 a.m. -- July 22 -- Flora

Dear Sweethearts:

I have come to the close of a long day. We left our rooms at 8:30 a.m. and went to a meeting in Osaka, after which we visited Rev. Nishihara our supervising pastor and Mrs. Nakashima our Pastor's wife who is still in the hospital, did some shopping before eating supper of hamburger and rice and coming back to Oji. We got back to our rooms about nine-thirty tonight.

You will be interested to know I am having a hard job deciding on gifts. Today I bought 5 pretty silk Japanese fans. I thought that they were typically Japanese. Do you think all of the ladies would like a silk fan?

The Japanese also have some rather nice Lacquer-Ware. Do you think the ladies would like candy dishes or some other article in Lacquer-Ware? We talked about tea, but there is only horrible green tea here. I will have to wait to London to get some exotic blends, if that is what I bring for some of the gifts. I keep looking for silk. It is very scare and not very pretty to me. I never did care for pongee. Some of the shantung is quite nice. The raw silk and the brocade look sort of useless to me. I would like your thoughts on these 4 kinds of silk.

Also, today I bought this Japanese fountain pen. My ballpoint that I swear by practically stopped on me. I do not know whether it is the paper here or the weather or what. The Japanese are famous for good inexpensive fountain pens. Should I buy each of the children one as a souvenir from Japan? I have also been thinking about buying the children some Japanese "Geta" shoes made of wood. This is just as a novelty and a remembrance of Japan. What do you think of these ideas?

By the way, I received my first Japanese haircut today. I was beginning to need one. The Japanese are such funny industrious folk. The barber purred over me like a kitten trying to figure out how I wanted it cut and then went straight to work. His old clippers were dull and ratty. He finished up with some hand clippers on the fine points. When he finished he sprayed me with some strong toilet water. I smell something wonderful and look fair, I think. All of this cost 100 yen, about 28 cents. Guess that I can afford another haircut or two before the summer is over.

Guess I had better write on the side, too. I get more mileage out of these aerogrammes than anyone in Japan. They cost about 13 or 14 cents here. Yours are cheaper. (ed. note: an aerogram or aerogramme is a thin lightweight piece of paper used for writing a letter and transmittal via airmail at a preferential rate.)

I noticed in the last letter I got from you, you asked about my Inn. Did I tell you about the Inn up on the mountain and how we had to ride the cable car to get up there? If not, remind me to tell you, also about the drinking parties, the old lady who tried to hug me, etc.

Sorry to hear about Brother Fox. Yes, he was retired but he served a small charge near Mt. Vernon. Brother Winn will have to find another part-time pastor.

Wendell wrote me again, also Brother Dycus. I wish you could read Brother Dycus' letter. Bless his heart; he keeps me up on all of the Conference news. That is good. I appreciate it greatly. Wendell wrote me from Cape Cod. They had visited Washington and New York and were planning to go on to Nova Scotia. They were in their camping trailer. They seemed to be enjoying it. That reminds me, you asked about a camping trip in September. It looks as though we could do that if you wish.

Well, I hope that you are getting along well with all of your responsibilities this summer. I look for a letter every two or three days. Ernie and Wendell know the value of mail. That is why they write, I think. Please write your ideas on the gifts suggestions. Also, do you suppose Mrs. Vallow wanted egg-shell or just a good china tea set? I had forgotten they had egg-shell till I got here. Hugs and Kisses to all, Walter

July 25, 10 p.m. Tokyo
At Flora, July 24, 5 a.m.

Dear Guys:

I have just returned from one of the best days that I have had in Japan. We had a district meeting of the American workers of the Lacour team in this district of Japan held at Kobe. It was very good to get away from the center and to see our fellow workers. We had a great time sharing experiences and laughing over some of our mistakes.

After the meeting, we had time to shop around a bit before returning home about 9 p.m. I bought 3½ yards of beautiful white silk shantung with a small black figure. I looked it over after getting here to see if it was as nice as I thought at the store. It bears up under inspection. It cost a little over $5.00. I also bought, or attempted to buy a Noritake tea set with service for twelve. I got twelve cups and saucers, a tea pot, and a cream and sugar bowl, but when I got home I realized that I do not have the twelve salad plates. I can get them later. What I did get cost almost $8.00. I hope that I can get them home safely.

When I got to Kobe, Dr. Lacour had my long lost box of food. The boys had tried to save me postage by bringing the box in the truck, but when they were in Oji two weeks ago they forgot to give it to me. Everything was safe. The glass jars of coffee not only came across the ocean but bounced around for over two weeks in the Lacour truck over terrible roads here. I stacked up the food, sat down beside it, and took a picture. Did it look good? I am going to start feasting on it tomorrow. No rice tomorrow. All of my packages have come now. I have sent one package home, just to try. It had some fans, chopsticks, and several small trinkets. Let me know if they deliver it before I get home.

Kikuchi-san, my interpreter, just came to my door and told me that our land lady reported that Mrs. Nakashima underwent surgery today. She has been in the hospital for twelve days and was not getting better. We hope that she will improve now.

I would like to see Mark do the dead man's float. I'll bet that he really can swim before I get home. When I returned home tonight I had a letter from you and one from Mom (ed. note: Walter's mother.) She said they were bringing Bud home and you say he is at home. Mark will have someone to

132

play with now. With the Etchisons moved, Bud and Mark will have to play more together (ed. note: although only five years old at the time, I remember wondering what happened to my playmate from next door.) *Hope Kaye and David are having a good summer. Hope David's team is doing better now. I see by the paper that the Cardinals have dropped out of first place, but today they appear only one game behind. That is really close. You asked about a newspaper. There is no paper here, but I subscribe for the Japan Times in Tokyo. I get it every day, even Sunday. It is a big help. I did not get a radio. The cheapest ones cost about $20 and I want to spend my money for other things.*

In the letter I got today, you asked several questions. I see it was mailed July 19. I think that I have answered most of them about pastor, interpreter, Inn, etc. The weather here has been very rainy. It has rained every day, yes every day. The sun has almost always shone some, but not long at a time. The temperature has not been too high. However, with the high humidity, my little fan sure has felt good. I have not used it for the last two days and last night it was positively cold.

I got my chlorine tablets and use them every day. There is no water system here in Oji and I am afraid of well water with those open sewers. I also got my vitamin tablets in the box of food today. I have already taken one of them. I think that I wrote you that the food is just as "bad" as reported. However, I am feeling fine. Less food does not hurt me any. I might get you the recipe for sushi, but you would not like rice wrapped in fish skins. The restaurant where we eat is trying its best to give us "western" food, but it is neither American nor Japanese.

I am going to get me a gas burner and go to work on this dried soup and lunch meat. The Japanese bread and pastries are good, so I ought to get along well.

Concerning the tea, Wow! Just like the rest, horrible green stuff. I will try to get some nice black tea somewhere. They say it is not here.

Concerning our location, Oji is in a little valley. A nice river runs around the town and there are mountains all around. Every day when we start to town, Kikuchi-san looks up and says "Oh, beautiful Japan." Out of my apartment window is a mountain, but it looks snaky and weedy, a sort of wilderness.

Glad to hear that the youth are going well. We have a fine bunch of youth here. They are the hope of the church everywhere.

Tell Debbie to be a good girl and not to run away with everything or break everything. Kaye was a bad one at that age. I believe her mother had to watch the pots and pans, etc.

I wonder if you got my letter to the pastors out yet. Send one to everyone that you can think of and don't forget the Bishop. I sent the letter to Max about a week ago. I hope that it is not too much trouble for him. I want to write one more just about the end of the work here and just as they return from California. By the way, I take it for granted that you think it best not to try to ship china? Max mentioned it insistently in his letter. What do you think? Let me know soon, for I believe that it is cheaper here than Tokyo. I hope that you are keeping my letters. Please answer the questions in the last two or three.

Give all of the kids a hug for me. My deepest love to you all. Continue to pray for our work here. Sincerely, Walter

July 26, 4 p.m. -- Tokyo
At Bunker Hill -- July 25, 1 a.m.

Dear Dad and Mom:

I received your letter a day or two ago. It was good to hear from you. Mail is scarce and very welcome out here. I am glad that Buddy could stay a week with you, and with no playmates that is probably long enough.

Missionary Letters from the Far East
By Walter

The pastor here at my center loaned me his typewriter so I am writing several letters on it. I think the best is to give you a quick rundown on the trip and experiences thus far.

We had a good trip to Chicago. The kids seemed to enjoy the city, airport, etc. Our party gathered in two groups. Part of us started from Chicago and the rest joined us at San Francisco. There are twenty-three preachers and five wives.

We road all night on the plane from Chicago to San Francisco. It was uneventful except over the mountains there were some thunder showers that made the air bouncy. I slept for about three hours of the eight hour ride. We had a nice breakfast at the San Francisco airport. It is truly a beautiful place, very new.

At about 9 a.m. we boarded a Pan American clipper; we had come from Chicago via United Airlines, and started out across the Pacific. The Golden Gate Bridge looked nice from the air. At 20 minutes beyond the point of no return one engine failed. However, there was no particular danger for it was a beautiful day and we had three other engines. Our speed was slowed down from 300 to 250 miles per hour. We made a perfect landing in Honolulu. We stayed one night to rest at the beautiful Reef Hotel. Hawaii is quite a place. I would like to spend a two-week vacation there sometime. It is a real vacation spot.

From Honolulu we boarded a Japan Airlines plane at about 8 p.m. Just at daybreak we arrived at Wake Island. It looks like a very small spot from 10,000 feet up. We landed and ate breakfast there. The weather was beautiful and the ocean was nice to look at all the way to Tokyo. It was quite an experience to look at the sunrise over the ocean. We arrived in Tokyo at a little after noon. A great crowd of Japanese Christians were there to welcome us. Their friendliness was heartwarming. Over and over again they said thanks for coming. They presented the ladies with flowers and took many pictures.

Missionary Letters from the Far East
By Walter

We stayed at the Imperial Hotel in Tokyo for a few days while we were given much instruction about our work. The first Sunday I preached in a Tokyo church and had the pastor interpret for me, my first such experience. It went better than I thought it would. The church elders gave a dinner for me. Wow, what a dinner. I did the best I could, not good, with Japanese food.

We then came to our centers. I have a little country town of about 10,000. Japan is crowded with people. We do have several shops and a doctor and a dentist here, but it is really a country town. There is no bank for instance. Tokyo and Osaka appeared very prosperous, but this town appears very poor. We had many welcome parties and have now settled down to the work. Evangelizing here is very difficult. We are in the heart of Shinto and Buddhist worship and converts to Christianity are hard to get. Don't let one tell you that we should let people go on in pagan worship.

We have Sunday school each Sunday at 9. Our average has been over fifty children and about seven adults. It is a thrill to hear the children sing and pray together. Both the pastor and his wife are wonderful with the children. The pastor plays the portable organ and a young man leads the children in singing. I tell a short Bible story each Sunday to them. We have worship at 10:30, average attendance is about 16. We have high school youth at 2 p.m. and evening service at 8 p.m. We have reception day on Wednesday. We invite anyone to come to see us that seem interested in Christ. Also, the members come. We have just six baptized Christians here not including the pastor and his wife. We hope to have several more at the end of the summer. There are 12 or 15 people that I would consider "earnest seekers" and the pastor has a list of about 70 more who have shown some interest in the church. There is a good chance for a church here. There is no other effort. We meet in a little rented room, but at least we have a place. This gives stability to the work. Soon we must buy land and make plans for a church. This is real pioneer work for Christ and church extension of the first order.

Missionary Letters from the Far East
By Walter

I have not visited Hatano, where brother Dycus was last year, but I am told there are even finer prospects. I did visit Ogu in Tokyo where Wendell and Wanda worked. They are now building a church which will be finished this summer. There the congregation pays the full support of the pastor already. The pastor's salaries are about 10,000 yen or $30 per month, if they are lucky.

We have had several other meetings with the folks here besides the Sunday services. We try to have some group meetings every day except Monday and Saturday. It is like a two-month revival of intensive effort. Pray for the success of our efforts. The harvest is ripe.

Hope that you are having a good summer. I hear from home every few days. They all seem all right. It will soon be vacation time. Sorry you are not going on a trip, but perhaps you will enjoy the trailer and the farm just as much.

Please write and give me lots of details. I welcome your letters and have lots of time to read them. As ever, Walter

July 29 -- 9 p.m. -- Osaka
At Flora, July 28, 6 a.m.

Dear Emma and all:

Well, we have gone through another week and half of my Sundays here are spent. The time is going by rather fast. Yesterday was not too good a day. It poured rain and our Sunday school was down to less than forty, our Worship was 21 thanks to several visitors, we had

Rev. Nakashima, 1957

10 at our high school meeting and only 7 at the evening service. We are doing our best to sow good seed, and there is interest. So we have faith for some harvest.

Today, Monday, we took the day off and went to Kyoto. Kyoto is the old capitol of Japan and the present Emperor was crowned there at the beautiful old palace. We saw castles, etc. as in Europe, but this one was different and very interesting. We also saw a famous Buddhist shrine, the Golden Pavilion, the university where our pastor graduated, Doshisha, quite a school with a total of about 15,000 students. It is the boyhood dream of Japanese to go to Kyoto. Many of the folk tales are built around a trip to Kyoto to seek one's fortune. As we left this morning, Kikuchi-san said, "Today, we are fulfilling one of my dreams." Neither of us was disappointed. We are very tired tonight from much walking, etc.

There are several things that I have been wondering about. Did Penny's ever call up to say that my wash and wear trousers had come. If not, forget it. Are there any District happenings? I received the letter about signing the papers for St. Elmo incorporation. They could have waited until September. Several of the men have written me friendly letters. They are Slow, Ragsdale, C.B. Johnston, and Martin. Evidently they got my letter from Martin, mimeographed and sent to them. Tell Brother Max that I very much appreciate this work. On second thought, they are gone to California now, aren't they?

It sounds as though Louisville Youth Institute is still on in Flora. Glad such great things are happening. The kids at Flora needed a spiritual revival and the older ones too. I hope that David and Kaye are profiting by this. I was glad that David went forward and committed himself to respond to God's call to any work that He should call him to. I do not want him to be a preacher just because I am, but I do want him to do what he feels God wants him to do with his life. Kaye has always spoken of missions. Here again, the place or the job is not as important as doing God's will.

Evidently Buddy had a short stay with Grandma. I hope that he and Mark are playing well this summer. School will soon start for both of them. Mark, you will like school, kindergarten, I am sure.

Have you had any accidents? I have been wondering. Usually we do not go this long without something happening. I received your letter today in which you tell about Debbie's bites. Why not spray the sand pile rather liberally. I imagine that is where she is being hurt. Tell Debbie that I would like to squeeze her.

Tell David that twice today I heard, "Walking in the Rain" over a radio. It must be popular here. The singer sings it in about half Japanese and half English. It sounds strange and interesting. Also, I get the newspaper and see the Cardinals' results about three days behind. In our paper today, Lindy McDaniel and Schmidt beat the Pirates in 10 innings and the Cards are 1/2 game out of first place. They are doing great, aren't they?

Concerning your letters, I believe that every one of them has now come through. I got them one and two a day, once they started. They were all forwarded to me. I was worrying about it one day and my interpreter said, "Don't worry, you will get them. You are the only foreigner around these villages." He was right.

Concerning the "Local Church Emphasis Kits," please write to Mr. Jones and tell him the situation, that I have these kits and that I will return them to him the moment I get home.

I have been to Osaka several times. Mrs. Nakashima is in the hospital there. We stopped by to see her this morning. She is getting along fine since surgery. We hope that she will be home within 8 or 10 days. There is not much silk cloth around here. The Japanese find it too expensive, and too, it must be dry cleaned. However, I have located a place in Kobe that has a fair supply. I will go there once more and try to get what you have requested, both in suiting and dress material. I have some nice blouse material.

Missionary Letters from the Far East
By Walter

Concerning the china, the home of Noritake Chinaware is Nagoya. It is about 2½ hour train ride from here. I plan to go there on Saturday, August 10. I will try to get you pattern number 5762; however, I need a second and a third choice. Counting the $100 that Dr, Lacour will return to me in Tokyo, I have enough money to buy two sets if they are not higher than I think. You spoke of trying to get some for Mom, Jim, and possibly the Martins. For each set I must have two or three choices on patterns and for every set over two that you wish, you must send me $50 for service for 8, 55 pieces, and $75 for each set over two sets, with service for 12, 93-99 pieces. I cannot make but one trip to Nagoya. My schedule is too full. It seems at the moment that August 10 is the only day available. If you answer right back, I will have your word in time. Remember that not all patterns are available, but I will do my best. Send both the number and the name, and more than one choice please. What do you think about the other gifts; fountain pens, silk fans, and Lacquer-Ware? These are available at about $1.00 each.

It is nice to hear from you so often. Tell the children that I enjoyed their letters, even Mark's marks. Thanks for writing. My love to you all. See you in my dreams. Walter

August 1, 7:30 p.m. -- Tokyo
At Flora, July 31, 4:30 a.m.

Dear Folks:

A few hours ago I started to write to you. Just as I sat down to write, the mail came. I had a letter from you and one from Brother Dycus. By the time I read and digested them it was time for supper. After supper I took a walk and since we have no evening meeting, I am writing earlier than usual tonight.

Missionary Letters from the Far East
By Walter

Brother Dycus reports a great time at Purdue and a plug for the Olney District by Mr. Vallow that was very good. He reports also that Mrs. Comer has undergone surgery, but is better and that Mrs. Attey and Mrs. Hendrix have been in the hospital. I get a big kick out of his letters. He was so homesick last year that it was a very bitter experience for him.

In your letter today dated...by the way, you never date them, postmarked July 27, 4 p.m., I observe that you give me the names and numbers of the Noritake china that you like. Apparently you, Lillian, and mom are the three who are interested. I have copied your numbers and pattern names down in my notebook and will do my best to get your first choice, also Lillian's first choice. I will get mom the same pattern that I get for you. I have found that it is best to send it in twenty-two pound parcels so that it will come by parcel post and be delivered directly to our post office. It will all have to be sent to me at Flora. I will declare it at the customs inspection and sooner or later we will get it. Each 22 pound package costs for postage about $6.00 and I believe that 3 packages will hold about 100 pieces of china. So you see the cost. The cost of the china itself varies greatly according to the pattern. I do not know what your patterns cost. The factory will tell me when I go there on August 10. If I am to get 3 sets of service for twelve, you had better send me $75. I believe that a bank draft can be cashed here. Ask the bank, but I believe Dr. Lacour can get it cashed here.

Since I wrote you last, we have had several meetings at our center. A caravan of girls from the Osaka Christian Center came over Tuesday and put on a fine program. They sang, gave some testimonies, and presented a short excerpt from "Uncle Tom's Cabin." It was good. One of the girls gave an illustrated story of Zacchaeus using a turned over chart of pictures that the girls had prepared. About 100 people were present. The girls gave a fine Christian witness. We really need it here.

Missionary Letters from the Far East
By Walter

I am praying and hopeful that some of them will become Christians. It is hard to break away from the old religions. They are thinking. The Holy Spirit will do His work I am sure. I have tried to be very kind and generous in my presentation. I appreciate your prayers much. Brother Dycus said that Mrs. Dycus had prayed for me that morning in their devotions and that he thinks of me and our work every day. This helps. I can see how the missionaries get discouraged, it's slow.

I think that I told you that we finally got our food. I took a picture of myself looking at it stacked out here on my desk. It looked wonderful. The gas man put in a small tank of propane and a gas plate for 500 yen, or $1.40. I have milk and rolls for breakfast, have wonderful soup and lunch meat for lunch, and hot or ice Nescafe any time I want it. Kikuchi-san really slurps my soup. I wish you could see and hear him. He loves this good "wester food," as he calls it. I tell him it is western all right, far west, cowboy style. I have bought a tea kettle, pan, dishes, etc. He says that we are "camping," and that he is greatly honored. Not even the Emperor has the privilege of being served by Dr. Smith. The restaurant sends in one meal a day. It is neither western nor Japanese, but we eat it. I don't believe I have lost any weight.

This week it has turned beastly hot. The rain has stopped and we are literally roasting in the heat and high humidity. My little fan is now working overtime. I did not use it at first. However, at night it gets nice and cool. I need cover before morning.

Today, a professor from Naperville UB Seminary visited us with a missionary from Osaka. They wanted to talk about evangelizing in rural Japan and about the struggles of a young church. Our pastor is a bright young man and answered their questions nicely. This afternoon they took us to a new sect in Buddhism. It is called Tenrikyo, literally Heaven sent truth. They have a spacious shrine which they claim to be the center of the Universe. They teach no morals; just that life is to be happy and joyous. The lady founder's spirit is supposed to hover about the shrine and inspire the faithful. There are several new sects in Buddhism and Shinto that have arisen since the war. Some of them stress faith healing, enlightenment, etc. The people flock to them. This shows the hunger of the people. They remind one of the small sects in American Christianity. They are our biggest competitors for people's minds. Anyway, it was an interesting experience.

Did I tell you that I have passage cleared to stop over in Calcutta, also a letter from Lee Memorial Mission saying that I can stay in their guest room on August 30th. Everything is working out beautifully for the trip around the world on the way back home. It would be wonderful if you were with me.

I will follow your instructions about the vase, the silk, the silk pictures, and the china. I have found beautiful tea sets in Kobe. You will love them. I have bought a pair of Geta shoes for each of the children, 5 pairs. I have also found some nice black tea. Can't decide how much of this stuff to buy. It is not expensive but it adds up and the postage is high.

Well, I must close. Give everyone a hug for me. I will write more later. I get a letter from you every 2 or three days. Thanks! With my love, Walter

August 6, 8 p.m., Oji, Japan
At Flora, August 5, 5 a.m.

Dear Mother, David, Kaye, Bud, Mark, and Deb:

Say, that is a mouth full, a typewriter full, too. Since you all are living the "life of Riley" this summer, you are peacefully sleeping and will be for about three hours yet. By that time I will be in bed too, the day ends as yours begin.

I got a letter yesterday and also one today from you. The one today is the typewritten one, which you must have taken about two days to do. Thanks for writing so faithfully. Mail is a real boon to life in these forsaken parts. I am getting along well, have a wonderful appetite thanks to my vitamin tablets, and the soup and luncheon meat is still holding out. One Japanese meal a day only isn't bad. I just felt and I still have my spare tire.

I wish you could see and hear us here sitting on the floor at our 15 inch high table. It is so hot that we wear as little as possible. We usually eat in our shorts. Every day Kikuchi, or Kikuchi-san as I call him, goes for a small piece of ice and we eat or slurp hot soup and swig iced Nescafe. It is "oishi," or delicious as the Japanese say. They really laugh at my speaking Japanese. I fool them some. I have picked up a few phrases like "Ohyaio gazaimus" or a very good morning and "sayonara" or goodbye. When I use their words they often respond in English, showing me how much they know. I have become an accepted foreigner with many of them, and I go along main street greeting and speaking to the merchants, standing out in front of their open shops.

By the way, I had better get down to business. There are a few things that I wrote down to tell you in my next letter. First, I received the clipping about the floods in Kyushu. It has certainly been very bad down there. We have no Lacour centers near there, as you probably realize. The latest reports are that there are about 1,000 known dead, perhaps others, and property damage running into the billions of yen. I noticed in the paper that the American Army, the American Red Cross, the American Church World Service, and the Christian Church were the first to respond in helping and with money. I had a good laugh in reading the Japanese paper. In large headlines it said Egypt gave 250,000 yen in relief to flood victims. There was a lengthy writeup. Below in small letters and a very brief paragraph it said the American Red Cross gave 3,600,000 yen, 14 times as much. Kikuchi-san explained it promptly. It is not news that Americans help us, but that Egypt helps that is "news."

Missionary Letters from the Far East
By Walter

Today, tomorrow for you is Kaye's birthday, remembered in Japan as one of the most terrible days in history. There is much in the paper today about the first atomic bomb which dropped on this day, 12 years ago. One report has it that 210,000 people were killed instantly and still, 12 years later, someone dies every week as a direct result of injuries sustained then. I wanted to go to Hiroshima today, but it is very far and I had no one to go with me. There is a peace foundation there that I would like to see. I hope that the Japanese will always hate war as they seem to now.

I went to Kobe yesterday to do a little shopping, and hope to go to Nagoya to finish up Saturday. I have now sent six packages home. I hope that you have no trouble getting them should they arrive ahead of me. Do not pay duty on them, but explain that I will declare them in Chicago on September 7 when I arrive.

What have I sent, well that is mostly known to you, but some secrets too, I hope. Everything is expensive here. I do not seem to get much for the money spent. I am not very well satisfied with some of the purchases after I get them, maybe they will do. They will be souvenirs, anyhow. I have not gotten the suit material or the necklace yet. Still debating, seems high. I hope to go to Nagoya where the Noritake factory is and get the china from there on August 10. I am a little worried about it, but hope that it can be done. I have your pattern names and numbers clearly in mind. The shipping worries me a little. Will let you know promptly how I come out with it.

Glad to know that David is mowing the lawn and keeping the car clean for you. Hope he has a good time at boy's camp. Kaye sure is getting a lot of badges and ribbons this summer. I haven't got it figured out when you go to Lebanon since you never give me dates or date your letters, but I take it for granted that it is this week. The children will have fun down on the farm camping with Granddad and grandma. Tell Debbie that I am glad that she still takes her nap. Take one every day.

I am glad to learn that you are having nice rains. Brother Chastain wrote me that all was well except that some farmers did not get out all of their crops because of too much rain. Your garden should be doing its stuff, the grass and weeds too.

Tell Mark that I like his idea about keeping the beautiful mountains. They are nice here in Japan. However, I got a real laugh at your suggesting my first Inn on the mountain was anything like Montreux. Wish you could have seen it, or better still smelled it. Wow!

Tell David that I am happy to learn that his team is doing better. Today's paper shows the Cards in first place by one game due to a win by Von McDaniel. Also, please tell him not to tease my Buddy so much. Bud, are you ready for school yet?

Well Kaye, HAPPY BIRTHDAY from half way around the world! I wish you "many returns of the day." My love to you all, Dad

P.S. Mrs. Nakashima is home after about 3 weeks in the hospital. We are glad. This and many other hindrances have slowed our work. She is doing well since surgery. She likes my soup.

August 10, 8:30 a.m. Tokyo
At Flora, 5:30 p.m., August 9

Dear Emma and all of the little friends:

Well, it is Saturday morning and soon I must prepare for Sunday. Before I do I thought that I would write you to say what has been happening during the last two or three days. Today I was supposed to go to Nagoya to visit the Noritake factory to buy the china. However, the man who was to show us around has gone to Tokyo on business and can't be there.

That ruins our plans. There is lots of china in Osaka, Kobe, and Tokyo and probably at just the same price.

I am sorry that I confused you on the price. I have not seen Noritake in the nicer patterns anywhere for less than fifty dollars plus shipping. The first information was that it could be shipped in a large box by freight. However, the man failed to tell me that it would come only to San Francisco and that I would have to pick it up there or pay someone to take it through customs and ship it on to me. This would be very expensive. By parcel post, it costs a little more but we receive it at our home post office. I still don't know exactly how much this would be, but I think 95 pieces could be placed in five 22 pound boxes. Each box of this maximum weight costs about $5.00. It still appears to me that you could do just about as well at Montgomery Ward. In my first letter about china, I think that I told you that it would cost $41 to $50 plus shipping, which I thought then would be about $20 per set. Anyway, it doesn't hurt to keep looking.

I have received two letters from you since writing the middle of this week. I appreciate hearing so regularly. The first was written on our Anniversary. I am sorry to have been away on this good day. As Brother Dycus said, "You and your family will have a nice vacation next year." He was telling me who was gone on vacation and about the Sims and Thetford going to Europe.

I have received several letters from home. Two came yesterday, one each from Wendell and Ernie. They are wonderful to keep me posted. I have heard also from L. B. Walkington, twice from

Walter with his Interpreter, 1957

Beaty, Barbara Campbell, and Harmon Dycus besides the ones I reported in the last letter.

*I intended to write to you last night, but I was too tired. We took the high school youth to the beach yesterday. It is less than one hour by train. They wanted to go early and stay all day. They rousted me out of bed before 7 a.m. and by 7:30 we were on the way. I bought a pair of trunks for about 60 cents and enjoyed the day with them. This was my first experience at so much swimming in salt water. We rented a plastic raft and played on it all day. There were ten of us altogether. The kids had a great time. We took our lunch and bought drinks on the beach and ate there. I asked one of the boys if we went early enough and he answered no. We got home about 6:30 p.m. and was I ever so sunburned and tired. I got out my unguentine (*ed. note: an over the counter topical antiseptic ointment*) and doctored up, laid around for an hour or so and decided that I was too sick and tired to write, so I went to bed. This morning it feels fine. In my other trips I got a good tan, but the sun hit some new places yesterday.*

I told you that Mrs. Nakashima is at home. However, she cannot take care of herself yet, much less do her work. The pastor must help her several hours a day. This has slowed our work down a lot. The Japanese have a hard timing seeing the importance of all of the work that we want to do. We are only here for eight weeks and want to be busy every minute. They have a life-time here. Still, we have a full schedule of some group activity almost every day and some calling two or three days a week. At the moment it looks very discouraging, but maybe a few will decide for Christ.

I enjoy all of the things that you tell me about the children. Everybody who writes says that it is extremely humid and hot. This is bad for "fatty" Debbie. Tell her "hi sugar" for me. Tell Mark that I slept for two nights on the airplane. From Chicago to San Francisco it was very "bumpy" and my first night I slept only about two hours. When I got in the plane I looked all the way down the strip to see if I could see the observation deck where I was supposed you were waving to me, but it was too dark. I couldn't see a thing. It was quite a lonesome sensation flying off into the night. We had a nice rest in Honolulu and when I got to Tokyo, I really slept. In my room here in Oji, I have a nice steel army cot and I sleep very well.

I guess that Bud is going to be our flute player. He remembers how to do it. Uncle Carl would be glad if Bud learned to play well I am sure. Kaye is sure making lots of clothes this summer. Every time I hear from you she is making another dress of some kind. She will be better dressed than a Japanese doll.

My paper yesterday still showed the Cards in first place, David. They had Monday off. I do not know what they have done since. You see, I get the news about four days behind in my paper. Mom hasn't said in the last two letters how your team is doing. Is it going bad again? She always tells me you have a lawn to mow.

I guess that you have the car radio fixed by now. Little things happen to them every now and then. However, ours hasn't done very well, has it?

I must close this lengthy epistle and get to work on my preparations for tomorrow. I have the morning service, a Bible story in Sunday school, a brief message in youth meeting, and I usually answer questions after the evening service. We had a dandy Bible class Wednesday. The youth really got down to business. Some of the questions about the Trinity, R. C. Protestant relationship, the meaning of the Cross, dropping A-bombs, etc. shows they are thinking. It also shows me how little I really know. Continue to pray for us daily. With all my love, Walter

Sunday, August 11, 9:30 p.m.
At Flora, August 10, 6:30 a.m.

Dear Emma and all:

Well church is over for another Sunday. We had about 40 children in Sunday school and I borrowed a tape recorder and made a tape of their singing, prayers, etc. It did not do too well but I thought that our children would enjoy hearing the Japanese. By the way, Mrs. Nakashima walked down to the church and stayed during most of Sunday school. She is slowly regaining her strength. I also made a recording of a little over half of the morning service. The pastor led the worship part as usual and I had the morning sermon today. There is about ten minutes of the sermon and you can hear how it sounds to preach through an interpreter. I believe that it turned out better than the Sunday school. We had only 12 in the morning worship and 6 at the evening service. With only six members I guess that this isn't so bad. Many more could come. We had 11 at the youth meeting today. They were the same ones that we took to the beach.

Speaking of the beach, my sunburn is getting better. I guess that I will peel some, perhaps not much. My back peeled off once this summer before I left home, remember. The first night I was miserable, like Kaye was that time she got too much at Shakamak State Park.

I received your $100 bank draft yesterday and another letter today. I will try to get it cashed tomorrow and see what my luck is. I have not bought the china yet, but I am still looking. I am planning to buy service for 12 for us in Alicia, if possible, and service for 8 for Lillian and mom in their first choice. The pastor is working on the possibility of buying it through a wholesaler. I doubt if this works out. I have had great problems choosing and buying the tea sets. They are bought and sent now. I hope to get a tea pot with our dinner set.

Missionary Letters from the Far East
By Walter

Tomorrow, Monday, is my day off. I plan to get up early and go to Awaji Island where we have a fine Methodist missionary named Gamblin. He will show us around his mission station. You can find Awaji in the bay out from Kobe and Osaka. It is the largest of the Isles there. This should be a fine experience. You asked about pictures. I am taking several, but how good?

I am glad that you got to go to Lebanon. I have heard that this Dr. Hirase is very good. I suppose that by now the school is over and you are home again. It will be interesting to compare notes on a foreigner's view of Japan and the native's that you will get. It is good that you got to visit Ernie and Geraldine. He paints the work here slow and hard. He is 100% correct on that. Only faith makes me hopeful that we will see any real decisions. Still, I am sure that there should be a church in this community.

You asked about where Oji was in relation to Osaka. I thought you could find it on the map in the boys' room. It is east and a little south of Osaka. We go through Osaka to Kobe. I refer to Kobe often because our meetings with the other workers have been there. Also, although Osaka is much larger, I enjoy going to Kobe much better. It is easy to get around there. Our only means of travel is by train. However, there is a train every thirty minutes or so and the fare is cheap. I can get to Osaka for 20 cents and to Kobe for 40 cents. I go about any time I take the notion and have time. That is not often, however.

I have heard from Ernie about the man at Flat Rock. Ernie is good to keep me up to date. He relieved Myers. If I had been there I would have given him a good talking to. He promised me faithfully that if I would get the salary up to $3,000 he would stay. He is one of those fellows that we took from another denomination and I am afraid that he is using the Methodist Church as an opportunity and does not really love us. Good riddance, perhaps! But I feel sorry for Flat Rock.

I have been receiving a lot of birthday cards and letters, is that the surprise to which you referred? The following have written within the last three days: Blessing, Milner, Chastain,

Simpkins, and Newcomb. It is good to hear from them all but I cannot answer them all personally.

I have wondered if the kids' cards ever arrived. I sent some by ship mail. They were some wood prints, nice cards, and some from Nara. These last have not come, I am sure.

You asked about the hospital. It is very crowded. The pastor's wife was in a room no bigger than mine, 9 by 12 feet, and there were two other beds in the same room. You walk in single file and almost literally back out. The cost was nominal compared to ours. It was about 1,200 yen, $3.25, for everything. Still, I don't see how Rev. Nakashima can ever get the bill paid. His salary is $10,000 yen per month, and he earns about 3 to 5,000 extra. 15,000 yen is only $40 per month.

Tell all of the kids hello for me and give each a big hug. Say David, my paper today says that the Cards are 1½ games back in 2nd place. The lowly Cubs have just beat them the second time in a row. I hope that your news is better up to date.

Kaye, how did you and grandma get along down on the farm camping? Bud, did you go to boy's camp or to the farm? Mother did not say. You could have a good time at either place. I know where Mark went. Granddad calls it "you farm," and Mark says "no, you farm." And poor Deb, she hates to be away from her mother, but Uncle James and Aunt Lillian showed her a good

Rev. Gamblin & His Church

time you can bet. It was good for mom to get to go to the school of missions. I hope that you all acted nice while she was away.

I must close this letter and go to bed so I can get up early tomorrow for a nice trip. I ride two hours on a boat. Wish you were here to enjoy it with me. My love to all.

Say, I will be leaving Oji after August 25. Do not address me here later than the morning of August 20. It would be nice to have a letter in Tokyo. The Christian News will deliver it to me at the Imperial Hotel. You could post a letter to me c/o Dr. Lardi about August 27. See you in my dreams, Dad.

7 p.m. -- August 13, 1957
At Flora -- August 12, 4 a.m.

Dear Guys:

By now you are well adjusted back into your home after a pleasant week away, I hope. You are no doubt glad to be home and all together again. I will join you soon as the time is flying. I have two more Sundays here, one Sunday flying across the Holy Land to Istanbul, and will be home before you know it. In some ways this has been a long stay, in others it has passed swiftly.

As I told you in my last letter Sunday night, some of us missionaries visited a mission station on Awaji Island Monday. It was a great experience. The man's name is Arthur Gamblin. He came to Japan first in the army of occupation. Here he met a fine Japanese Christian girl in his experiences in the church. He went back home and to Drew Seminary. The girl came to America to school. They were married and returned to Japan as missionaries, Methodists of course, and in May 1958 will finish their first five-year term.

He is in charge of all of the Protestant work on Awaji Island except a Free Methodist Church that will not cooperate. There are just four churches in his parish and three Japanese workers assist him. It was enlightening to hear him explain right here how mission works. I have come to have a greater and greater admiration for these missionary couples. You remember that on our trip to Europe we were not greatly impressed by some missionaries we met. When one considers all they go through, we must admire them. The Gamblin's have a nice home as my pictures show. I have my fingers crossed the pictures are good as it rained all day, but when you step outside, life is far from easy. He rides a motor scooter to the three out posts. The farthest one is 25 miles away and the roads are terrible.

I enjoyed the boat ride very much. One other missionary went with me. We were four hours on the water, 2 hours each way. When we got to the Island our ship was too big to go into the harbor and a small boat, very ancient looking with a one cylinder motor, came bouncing out over the waves to take us ashore. What an experience! I am very sorry that it was raining, my raincoat came in handy, I am afraid my pictures will be very poor.

I had to hurry home for an evening meeting here in Oji last night. I did stop in Kobe long enough to cash your $100 check. I had no trouble cashing it at the Bank of America and they charged me only about 25 cents for cashing it. It is not as difficult as I am making it sound. We have a heavy schedule here, and when we go away for the day there are always many things to see, so I sandwich my shopping in among many things of business and pleasure.

By the way, I bought the silk for your suit. It is a beautiful navy blue. The black I did not like so well. It was a sort of taffeta shantung. The blue is a nice shade and heavy shantung, perfect for suiting. You will like it.

Our meeting last night in the center was led by a famous Christian businessman of Japan, Mr. Momotani. He is the president of a cosmetics firm and the Japanese leader of Gideons. He gave a fine testimony. He told how he became a Christian forty years ago when the flu epidemic came. While he was sick, a friend gave him a copy of the New Testament. He was so impressed, though only a high school boy, he decided for Christ. He urged the people to give heed to our Christian mission.

So far, we have had two decisions (ed. note: people committing to Christ.) *We are hoping for several more. Tonight, the pastor and I counted up our reasonably good and earnest seekers. There were 12 names listed. Not all will be ready just now, but we are praying that we can at least double our membership. We started with six members; the pastor added one by transfer from another Christian Church that had actually decided before I came; now we hope for at least seven new ones, maybe more if our faith were stronger. We appreciate your prayers at home.*

That reminds me, I have received 12 birthday letters and cards. I never had it so good. The new ones are Hearn, Watson, Hooper, Bishop, Longberry, Pinkstaff, and Stoneburner. I think that I want to celebrate my birthday next year over here. I have nice birthdays at home, but not so many people pay attention to me as when I am here. They are a very pleasant surprise.

For three days in a row I heard from you, now for three days there has been no letter. That is the way your letters come. I am wondering if that is the way you write or if that is how the letters make mail connections. Anyway, I have heard often and I am glad that you write so faithfully. A letter will come tomorrow.

I just went to look at my notebook. I was thinking that there was some business that I wanted to tell you. There seems to be nothing important in this little book. The Nakashima's came in for a conference and for iced Nescafe. It is now after 10 p.m. We are looking for Dr. Lacour's second visit to our center on Friday night. He will help us with our seekers. We were making plans for serving them the evening meal and getting the seekers all to attend the meeting. We have complications. This is the week of Buddhist holidays and Oji has a big display of fireworks, etc. right on Friday night. Our pastor did not realize this until it was too late to change the date. We have had many things just like that all summer it seems. Still we have had much to be thankful for.

There is just a little space left to say "hi," which by the way means "yes" in Japanese, to all of the kids. Dave, our poor Cards have now skidded in my paper to 4½ games back. You are not rooting hard enough. I bought a simple Japanese doll for the girls. Wish I could see my Bud and Mark and carry them to bed tonight. And of course, I wish I had a big kiss from my mom. Glad you are all well. Each of my birthday letters mention something about you. That sounds good to me.

I know now what the business referred to above was. It was about meeting me in Chicago. I will discuss it in my next epistle. With love to all, Walter

August 15, 1957, 9 p.m.
At Flora, August 14, 6 a.m.

Dear Emma, David, and all:

I especially address David because I have received his letter from boys' camp and I liked it very much. Dave, I am glad that you had such a good time both physically and spiritually at the camp. How did your team do while you were away at camp? The Cardinals have done bad, having lost 6 in a row. I hope your team has done better. I am glad that you are taking some part in the services at camp and at your youth services at home. Your Bible reading and Upper Room will help you grow in your faith.

We have some wonderful children and young people here. We have just returned from a farm home where we went this afternoon with a group of 6 high school youth and ate supper and held a home meeting. They all had a good time and the farm family really fed us. The mother, bless her heart, tried her best to give me a "wester meal" as they say. The rest ate some kind of noodles with mushrooms, soya sauce, red beans, and cucumbers. I am sure that it was good by the way they sounded eating it. I had fried eggs and potatoes with sweet bread and grapes and peaches, fresh ones, for desert. Not bad, I still feel very full. It was a nice experience.

This morning we went calling as we often do. We visited the lady who has made her decision for Christ. She is so happy and is anxious for the Baptismal service on August 25th. The pastor wanted to explain something about the meaning and the service, also how to meet all of her relatives, some of whom are strong Buddhists. When we were about to leave, she told me how happy she was and went and got a Japanese doll. She asked me if I liked it and she promptly put it in a box for me. I shall treasure it as a gift from our first convert in Japan. We have three now and are praying definitely for several more. We hope to have some to Baptize now and a class of others to meet with the pastor for instruction and prayer until Christmas to be baptized then. We are praying that we may have all six of the youth we took to the farm and home today. It is very hard for them, coming out of nominal Buddhist homes. I thought today how different from America. There the leading citizens are often Christians and the church is a respected organization. Here the mayor and all of the leading citizens are Buddhists or some sect of Shinto and the church is thought of as a poor weak concern. It is here as it was in the earliest days of New Testament Christianity.

I received a wonderful letter from Bishop Brashares saying that he has heard from you and encouraging me. He is taking a brief vacation in Michigan, staying at a placed marked "for elderly people." He says that he and the Mrs. are about the only ones there. He tells of ripe peaches and blueberries just to lure me home as soon as the work is finished here. He also gave me a subject for Pere Marquette. He is a dandy. I will try to preserve his letter for you to read.

Missionary Letters from the Far East
By Walter

In my last letter I said that this time I would make a suggestion about your meeting me in Chicago on September 7th. My thought is this. See what you think. Why not get up real early, say about 3 or 3:30 a.m. and drive to O'Hare Airport to meet me. I will arrive around 8:30 a.m., but by the time I claim my baggage and fill out all of the custom paper and have cleared, it will be at least 9:30 a.m. perhaps even 10:00. The O'Hare Airport is on Route 45, just west of Chicago. If you stay on Route 45 all of the way you cannot miss it (ed. note: O'Hare Airport is so large today that "missing it" seems incomprehensible.) *There is a very large sign pointing to it along the highway. You can drive from Flora there in 5 or 6 hours that early in the day because for most of the way traffic will be light. You may even miss the biggest rush in Kankakee and La Grange if you do not get there until 10. We can then drive home easily before night. Perhaps you can get someone to come to stay with the kids throughout the day. David can be their bodyguard until they all awake. What do you think of this? If you do not wish to come so far to meet me, I will telephone you about where to meet me closer on that day, September 7.*

I am getting anxious to clear up many matters here and be ready when closing day comes. We have a full schedule until then. The Lacours will be here tomorrow night for their closing night. They will help us to "draw the net." Each day we have someone to see and talk with personally. We have youth retreat for three days next week and I would still like on my day off next week to go to Hiroshima to the Peace Park. I would also like to see the Christian center in Kobe and the home of Mrs. Nabuko. There are too many things to see and too much important work to do here for me to reach the souls that we must work on.

Mrs. Nakashima is gaining strength every day and the pastor can now give more time to help and guide me. This makes our work accomplish more. We must see many people and talk long and slowly to win some. However, I believe that the Holy Spirit goes ahead of us and prepares the hearts of the people. Continue to pray. Now is a crucial time. We will have our Baptismal Service on August 25.

I would like to use this last part of the aerogramme to say a few words to the children. Have you noticed? I have already spoken to David. However, I did not ask him how the ping-pong tournament came out at camp. Sounds like you, Brownie, Brothers Howard and Murphy are pretty good buddies. By the way, how is my Buddy? I have bought him something he will like. If I haven't told him in another letter, let's keep it a secret. Kaye and Deb are my two best girlfriends. There are lots of little girls in Kimonos (ed. note: traditional Japanese formal garments worn for important celebrations and occasions) *downtown tonight as part of the celebration, Buddhist Christmas. They are cute, but not as cute as you. Hi there Mark. I wish you could see the beautiful mountains of Japan. The rice fields, vineyards, peach orchards and tea groves are beautiful. Then above them tower the mountains. I guess that I should not forget to throw a kiss to mother. She deserves it for staying at home to take care of all of you this summer. I enjoyed her letter on Japan. It came today. The slant on Japan is interesting and for the most part true. With love to all, Walter*

August 18, 11 p.m.
At Flora, August 17, 7 a.m.

Dear Kougas:

As Debbie says, "Hi Kouga." I received your card and letter today with her picture in it. Several times I have been asked to show pictures of the children and I must explain that I do not have a billfold size picture of her yet. She has certainly grown and changed. She already looks like a young lady and no longer appears as a baby. I am sure that you all have changed a lot during these ten weeks.

Well, we are through another Sunday. We had 48 in Sunday school, 15 in Worship, 12 in the youth service and only 4 tonight. However, I think that this last was providential. We had a lady present that has been on the top of our prayer lists. She is about 50 or so and the most influential person we have been able to get to our services. If we could win her, perhaps more could be won. We had a chance to talk to her for about one hour about Christ and the Church. She is interested in a most serious way. She had an aunt who was a Christian, so she knows something about Christianity.

We are now approaching our last week here in Oji. Next Sunday will be our last service with baptisms and communion service. This will be our most fruitful week. I am hopeful that several will either be baptized now or join the pastor's class for baptism at Christmas. The work is slow, but it is moving. In America it is impossible to realize how great a victory those three we have won already are. If we get three or four more this week that will double the number of Christians we found here at the beginning of the summer. Continue to pray. Within a few days I will leave Japan, but I will never lose my interest in these fine children and youth in Oji. They have a long, hard step to come to Christ. A few have the courage and understanding to do it. Only eternity will tell the full story of this pioneer work. They can give stories of rather sizeable numbers in cities like Osaka and Kobe, but 10 is a big number here.

Everyone says that the last week is the most rewarding one. We are to it now and I am anxious and prayerful approaching it. Wendell and Ernie think it will be fruitful and our prayers answered. Sometimes my faith is strong and again weak as I face it close up. I will write again and keep you up to date.

I have not bought the china yet. I may have to wait until I return to Tokyo. I am not worrying much about it now. We have a heavy schedule of services and interviews for this week. Tomorrow we go to a youth retreat. Seven of our youth are going. We will talk to them and pray with them there. Only two in the group are Christians. When we return Wednesday, we have a list of interviews, a children's meeting, and a home meeting to round out the week's schedule before the last Sunday.

Tomorrow on the way to youth camp, I will stop in Osaka to make one last effort there to buy the china. If it fails I will try in Tokyo. I feel sure that it can be obtained there and properly packaged for parcel post.

I have had a wonderful birthday. Yesterday, I received 7 cards and letters and today I received 8 more. Altogether, I have received more than 20. Most of them do not say much, but they show a wonderful interest and friendship. I have appreciated them very much. "Domo Arigato" as they say in Japanese. Yesterday, I took my day off for the last week and went hurriedly to Hiroshima. Many things were disappointing about it, but I did see the city, the Peace Park, the memorial, and museum, but not the mission school. It was a miserably hot day. The train was sooty and dirty. Last night on returning, I was black as a piece of coal and Kikuchi-san thought I looked a little like a drunk. Mr. Dorsey, my roommate, agreed to take a group of us early in the period, but when he learned Tanimoto-sensei, the guide was not there. He said there was no use for we had no contact there to show us around. At the last moment I went alone. It was not too satisfying, but worthwhile. I am glad I went. I just hope that my pictures turn out well. I have also taken many pictures here of our center and our home. The Lacour's were here Friday night for their last visit. We had our supper sent in from the restaurant and I served a few extras, such as orange juice, sliced peaches and Nescafe. I took a picture of Dr. Lacour helping Mrs. Nakashima with dishes after supper. I must take a picture of me doing the dishes here, too.

Among my letters today was a letter from mom. She is always very brief. She did say that they enjoyed the children down at the farm. She said that she told Mark to say "Good Morning, Daddy," every night as he went to bed. I imagine he got a smile out of that.

I also have another letter from both Ernie and Wendell. They are faithful to keep me up on the news. Although I have written Maurice, he has not responded. He went on a month's vacation about ten days after I left and is just getting home, I think.

Well Dave, the Cardinals have "run out of gas." In my paper today it shows that they have lost eight straight games, but still are in second place. What is wrong? I still think of your letter. It was good to get it. I imagine that Kaye is anxiously awaiting school to start, no? She will then get to wear all of her nice new fall dresses. Bud and Mark will soon have to quit swimming for this year. It does not seem possible that fall could be so near.

I have just reread your two letters to see if there is anything I have not answered. The only thing is that I have not received the birthday package yet. If it is something to eat, I hope it arrives in good shape. All of my other things did. The Japanese will enjoy a "feast" with me. They love American food. I have just one can of meat and 5 packages of soup. Good thing it didn't come earlier. I share it with the Nakashima's daily. She is gaining strength. My love to you all "Good Morning" Mark, et. al. Dad.

Oji, Nara-ken, Japan
August 22, 1957, 10 a.m.
At Flora, August 21, 7 p.m.

Dear Folks:

Well, our mission here at Oji is drawing swiftly to a close. We leave here Sunday night after the service bound for Tokyo and arrive there about 7 a.m. Monday. I want to go to Ogu again to take some pictures for Wendell, to Kamakura to see the big Buddha, to International Christian University, and do some shopping in Tokyo. I have my final personal conference with the Lacours on Monday at 4:30 p.m., Tuesday is free, and Wednesday we have an all-day farewell meeting, summary, etc. with all of the Japanese workers. These dates are August 26, 27, and 28. I leave for Hong Kong about midnight on August 28. Did I tell you that I received a wonderful letter from Sidney Anderson of Hong Kong saying that he would show me around? He is a Methodist missionary there. I also have a letter from Walter Griffiths at Calcutta with an invitation to stay in the guest rooms at Lee Memorial Mission and he promises to have someone to help me see our work and the city. I have also another letter from Dr. Lardi saying they had a wonderful trip to Switzerland and looking forward to our visit to Epworth Youth Institute, etc.

Things are moving, if only slowly here at Oji. We took six youth and went to a youth retreat at a large mountain home, August 19, 20, and 21. We all had a great time. It was nice and cool up in the mountains and the scenery was just magnificent. We started each day with a sunrise service, open air, followed by breakfast, Bible study, discussion groups, group singing, and lunch. In the afternoon was recreation, hiking, vesper and supper. After supper, there was a very impressive camp fire service, where kids gave testimonies, etc. The eating was strictly Japanese, wow! We slept (?) on the floor and generally enjoyed ourselves. It was a little hard on an old man. I was glad to get back into my bed last night where I slept 10 hours.

We now have 5 new members. The number is gradually climbing. We are praying for four more of our youth who have not yet accepted Christ. With the six they got last year, 1 that Rev. Nakashima got early this summer, and our 5 more, we now have 12 Christians in Oji. That does not sound like much, but that is a great victory for this place. We must have two or three more before I leave.

I had a most wonderful birthday. The surprise was great. I can scarcely imagine how Debbie has changed. She looks smiley, too. There have been 34 pastors of the Olney District who have written to me or sent birthday greetings. Besides these, I have heard from all District Superintendents and several others, including three lay people from Lawrenceville. I also appreciated the children's notes on the letter and Mark's marks.

The garden sounds wonderful. Glad you like your green beans, tomatoes, peppers, etc. I would enjoy the flowers, too. Kikuchi-san has taught me the importance of stopping when you are 80% full, but I am thinking that I would slurp up beans just like Debbie if I were there. Glad that you are keeping the weeds pulled. With just a little raking, grass can be sown and the back lawn will look nice next summer for the new residents of 210 W. 12th Street. By the way, did I tell you that Ernie told me that J.O. Hall was talking for Farrell and against his pastor as District Superintendent for next year? These laymen are exercising themselves these days. I am afraid that no one knows who the new man will be and it is early to discuss it, I think. The Bishop will meet us at Pere Marquette and will want to begin thinking, I am sure. All I want is harmony.

Say, I heard that Victor Norris got married. I am glad. He will make Bible Grove a good man. His wife seems very nice.

I am sorry to hear about Jim and Lillian's troubles. I guess that we could have caused a lot of trouble when Kaye was hurt. I am glad that we didn't. However, I do not see why Jim must sign over the house if they have insurance. This is why I pay insurance premiums, to protect what little we have. I would not sign anything until after the litigation is complete if I were them. Glad that Charles and Loretta have a house.

Missionary Letters from the Far East
By Walter

You have spoken several times about wishing you could come to Japan. In some ways it would have been wonderful, but for the most part, I am glad that you didn't. Life is rough in rural Japan, especially under circumstances like this outside an Inn. You couldn't eat in these restaurants. They would turn your stomach inside out. If it hadn't been for this American food to give me an appetite, I would have lost 25 pounds. Mrs. Nakashima being gone and the worry over the children would have been too hard to make it worth it. I joke about it, but it is no joking matter really. Glad my food didn't come early. I have just 3 packages of soup left and one can of meat. We will stretch it for three days. That will leave only Sunday. To go back to the restaurant now, ugh!

I think that it would be nice for you to go to Grandma Smith's for a few days before school starts. They seem a little lonely in their new place. I have had two more letters from them. I am afraid that dad is not very well. Dave can miss another game if he needs to and the others, other things. I am beginning to realize that we are not going to have them with us always, our folks I mean.

Well Dave, my paper shows the Cards took the Braves 3 out of 4 games but are still far behind. Kaye, I hope that you enjoyed the girls from Olney, also that you and Dave are having a good time at church. Buddy and Mark got plenty dirty down on the farm, grandma said. She likes to see you play. Did she make you sing "Abbra Kadbra, Debbie is a sweetie pie?" and so is mom.

I send my love to you and shortly I will bring it in person, I hope. What have you decided about meeting me in Chicago? Love Dad

P.S. I heard about the Missionary Rally September 10. I am afraid that I have given up on your dishes. They are not available in Japan, I fear. I am very sorry to hear about Crackel. I feared this when I saw him last.

Oji, Nara-ken, Japan
August 24, 1957, 10 p.m.
At Flora, August 23, 7 a.m.

Dear Emma and all:

Well, our prayers have been answered! We have had a surprisingly fruitful ingathering for our last service tomorrow. We shall receive 10 new members into the church. Seven will be baptized. One week ago it looked hopeless; we were cautiously hoping for 4 or 5 and praying for more. We have reached all of our people who were ready and the pastor will have a class beginning in October for 5 or 6 more that we have worked and prayed with this summer to be baptized at Christmas. Ten does not sound like many, but when you consider that none of these come from Christian homes and the percentage of increase, it is truly a great victory. With only 6 to begin with and now 17 counting the one the pastor received by transfer just before I came, it certainly encourages this little courageous, but struggling group.

Tomorrow, we have the last service here. It will be a baptism and communion service. They also want me to preach, but there will be little time for that. I am very happy. I know that this victory is the result of the great volume of prayer that southern Illinois raised in my behalf here.

Tomorrow evening the Oji people plan a farewell service for Kikuchi-san and me. I do not know just what it will be like. We had a whole series of welcome parties in Tokyo, Kobe, and here and now starts the farewells, one here and one in Tokyo on Wednesday. I am a little afraid that the people will load me down with a lot of knick-knacks. They have all been very wonderful and have tried in many ways to show kindness and appreciation. I am thinking that I will have to send another package from Tokyo. I have sent 7 different parcels to date. One went out about one month ago and the last one today.

166

By the way, I failed to completely find any of your patterns of china. They are all for export, only.

Back to our joy at these new people who have accepted Christ. We took 6 youth to camp as I told you. Two were already Christians and all four of the others have made their decision. This sounds a little like home. The pastor is almost overjoyed.

After the farewell service that lasts from 7 to 8:10 or so tomorrow evening, the whole congregation will walk us down to the railway station. At 8:51 p.m. we catch an express for Tokyo. It is the custom here to meet guests at the station if you know when they are coming and by all means to see them off all the way to the station when they leave. Sometimes the stations are very crowded and you wonder where everyone is going, then you realize that about 2/3 of them are there to see guests off. When I arrived here in Oji, Kikuchi-san was very careful that we came on the exact train suggested so that the members could meet us at the station, and quite a group of them were there. It is impossible to describe the way they take you in and determine to take care of you while you are here.

I am very happy about the summer in spite of the many discouragements, but I am also very glad to start back to Tokyo. It is good to go in a sense that your work is at least done for now and that the church is strengthened. It is also good to think of having the conveniences of "wester life" again. One of our team members wrote in our newsletter, thinking of the Imperial Hotel, "Breathes there a man with soul so dead, he hasn't wished for an Imperial bed." Although I haven't lost much weight, if any, I am looking forward to better food. Say, yesterday Kikuchi-san and I went to the restaurant. He ordered "soupa" or soup, black noodles and soy sauce, and I ordered two fried eggs, rice for bread, and fried potatoes. Usually these are clean and fairly fresh. In nothing flat, Kikuchi-san received his noodles and I had two eggs. I waited but no rice or potatoes came. *Five minutes passed, then ten. By this time Kikuchi-san had slurped down his noodles and was getting about ready to go or order something else. He looked over at me and said, "Why don't you eat your eggs?" I responded that I had nothing to eat them with. About that time they brought the silverware and the potatoes. I never did get the rice. In the meantime I employed Kikuchi-san by having him order more noodles. Today we ate the last of our soup and luncheon meat. Tomorrow, we go to the restaurant for more noodles, sushi, etc., and then to the Imperial Hotel.*

I have my room hanging full of washing tonight. Do you remember how I washed on our trip to Europe? Well, I wash something about every day. But, tonight I had an unusually large wash trying to get everything ready to pack up.

I received your "blue Monday" letter today. Sounds like the joy of your freedom and the use of the car every day is getting a little old. I will soon be home to put you really to work again. Things will "pop." Missionary Rally on the 10th, Pere Marquette the next week which I hope you can go, my group quarterly conferences, meeting galore, I fear. Mom said in her letter that I would never get caught up. Say, 36 Olney District pastors have written or sent birthday cards.

To the kids, I enjoyed David's remark that my coming home soon "Is a good deal." When you get this letter, you will already be back in school, I guess. I hope that Mark likes kindergarten and I know he will. I sure do like Debbie's new picture. She surprises me in changing so much in such a short time. Good night to all of you, or is it good morning, "I see you in my dreams." Good morning mom, too. With all my love, Dad

P.S. This will be my last letter on Nakashima, sensei's typewriter.

Missionary Letters from the Far East
By Walter

Oji, Nara-ken, Japan
August 25, 1957, noon
At Flora, August 24, 9 p.m.

Dear Friends of the Olney District:

I have just come from one of the greatest services of my life, which was climaxed with Holy Communion. Two weeks ago, no one could have persuaded me that there would have been this victorious conclusion to our summer's work. I feel sure that it has come as an answer to the great volume of prayer you raised in behalf of our work and mission here.

Remember that we started the summer finding six Christians here? They were greatly discouraged, almost despairing. The pastor added one member by transfer just before I arrived here and today, by the Grace of God, we added eleven more. This means that since our first report, the group has been strengthened by exact 200% in numbers, and in spirit, the increase is even greater. Ten today here in Oji is equivalent to one hundred in a sizeable county-seat town in our Conference. What a victory that would be! The pastor, Rev. Nakashima is overjoyed.

Speaking of him, I would like to tell a little about him. He graduated from seminary last April and was stationed in this mission. He is twenty-five years of age, is married, and lives in a one-room apartment here in the same building where I am staying. Both Rev. Nakashima and his wife are excellent workers and determined to raise a church here in Oji. I wish that you could see them work with the children. The pastor plays our little portable organ and away they go with the singing. The youth work is just as inspiring. We took six of our youth to camp last week. Two of them were Christians, but today the other four were baptized and were among those ten received into the church. Sounds like home!

Missionary Letters from the Far East
By Walter

I believe that I told you that we have rented a building on the main street where the church meets. It is very inadequate as my pictures will show. But, this little struggling group will never get a church unless we help them. The first need is for land. We have looked at and priced some sites. It will take $5,000 to buy a location, even a small one. Japan is very crowded and land is very expensive. The church that the Carbondale District built in Tokyo cost $5,000. It looks very nice and would serve Oji well. But, $10,000 converted to Japanese money means 4,000,000 yen. You see how impossible that figure sounds to a small group, almost half of whom are high school youth. Yet, they have courage and faith that they can do their part and that it can be done. I am not so sure about my faith at this point.

Still, this has been a great summer. Thank you for sending me this way. I wouldn't have missed it. Surely after attending these children's services, our youth English Bible classes, the home meetings and all of the rest, I will be a stronger Christian.

Thanks also for the many letters and birthday greetings. I think that it would be good to celebrate another birthday here. I never had so many people paying attention to me. Never in my life have I received this many cards. They began to come at a low time. Mrs. Nakashima was in the hospital, our work was at a standstill, and the outlook was dark. Your cards and letters, mail always helps when one is away from home, gave just the inspiration needed to send us back to work again to "reap the harvest." The pastor will have several more to accept Christ and be ready for baptism at Christmas, I am sure.

Please forgive me for such a long letter, but I just had to share this victory with you. It is your victory, too. Tonight I leave for Tokyo. Wednesday, I leave Japan. Soon, I hope to look into your faces again. Until then, God Bless Us Everyone,
Walter A. Smith

Imperial Hotel, Tokyo
August 27, 1957, 10 p.m.

Dearest and all:

Well, I am back in Tokyo. Arrived here yesterday morning
and have been having a busy time. We, Kikuchi-san my
interpreter and I, left Oji at 9 p.m. Sunday and rode all night
on the train, but this Imperial bed helps you to get rested fast
compared to the floor, futon in Japanese, and the army cot.

We had a truly great closing out at Oji. I told you ten were
received into the church, but we received eleven actually. I miss
counted. We had eight on profession of faith and three transfers.
I have not talked with anyone yet who had that many, although
I feel sure some did, and more. Tomorrow is report day and
farewells. We shall get all of the figures then. Our work at Oji
was surely an answer to prayer.

The Oji church was really struggling for its life in June
as now with 18 members instead of 6 and it has really come
to life. What a farewell they gave us on Sunday evening. We
met at 7 p.m. at the church. Many people made speeches of
appreciation to us and to God. Most of the new converts were
speaking in public for the first time. It was a stirring time. At
about 8:30 p.m. we left the church as a body, they carrying
our bags and we marched very slowly and informally down the
main street. We had shopped in many of the markets and all of
the proprietors came out waving and saying "Good-bye." The
stores are open every day in Japan and until about 10 p.m. in
the country towns. At the train station each one of the 30 or
so people had to shake hands and speak of appreciation again.

The station attendant let them all come into the area near
the tracks where they began to sing, "God be with you until
we meet again." As the train left they ran alongside waving
and half-crying. It really pulls at your heart strings. Tomorrow

171

is the farewell for center pastors and interpreters. The Japanese are the greatest ever for welcome parties and farewells.

Since coming to Tokyo, I have had my last report meeting with the Lacours. They seemed pleased with our outcome. I did a little shopping for small articles. I got a cheap necklace and earrings. They are not very nice, but a souvenir. I looked again for Alicia Noritake. What I was told in Osaka is true. The 57 in your design number means 1957 and they are not available in Japan yet. The company sells them abroad for at least one year first.

I have sent seven packages of trinkets. You may begin to receive some of them soon. Also since returning here, I have gone out to Ogu again to see the Robinsons' new church. It is very nice. The day was cloudy, so I fear for my pictures, but maybe they will show something of how it looks.

Today, my interpreter and I went to Kamakura to see the big Buddha that everyone talks about. He is nice. This afternoon we went out to see the International Christian University. There we saw the dormitory for faculty women that our W.S.C.S built. They took me in and showed me Dr. Harkness' room. She taught here last year, I believe. Their student body is now up to 660 and this year they graduated their first class. Dr. Diffendorfer of our Methodist Mission Board was one of the founders of it.

Time has come to close again. Tomorrow night I go to Hong Kong. I may wait to write a letter from Calcutta. I will try to send a card from each place.

Tell all of the kids I am getting awfully homesick to see them. I hope David's team was successful. Just received your letter addressed to the Christian News. I hope you find Dr. Lardi's address. If not, okay. Glad the kids enjoy the prayer and church services so. Hope that you had a good time over at Bunker Hill with Granddad Smith. Now to start to school and in about 10 days, I will see you. My love to you all,
Walter

*P.S. Guess Brother Max is getting out my second letter. Give
him money for paper, stamps, etc.*

*Peninsula Hotel, Hong Kong
August 29, 1957, 8:30 p.m.*

Dear Emma and all:

    *Last night I boarded a Pan American Clipper about
midnight and arrived here in Hong Kong at 8:00 a.m. this
morning. It was a very pleasant flight. I did not remember
much about it.*

    *We had a really big day yesterday. These Japanese
welcomes and farewells really wear me out. All day from 9 to
3 we sat and listened to all sorts of reports as each center told its
story. In a way it was interesting for each had a different story
to tell. Each thought his was the most exciting and rewarding. It
was inspiring but 22 reports makes the day too long. We closed
with a communion service at 3 p.m. then all got in a taxi and
"raced" out to the airports. Wendell warned me when getting
into a 70 yen cab to close my eyes and say a prayer. He is very
right. I took Kikuchi-san and Nakashima-sensei with me as
they wanted so much to go. The larger portion of missionaries
left for Honolulu at 6:30 p.m. About 10 of us stayed behind
going other places. Five of us came to Hong Kong. Kikuchi-
san and Rev. Nakashima left for their homes at about 7 p.m.*

    *When midnight, 11:59 p.m. flight actually, came I was so
tired that I fell asleep instantly on the plane and did not awaken
until 6:30 a.m. as the Stewardess began feeding us breakfast.
We had a good breakfast of an omelet, pineapple juice, toast,
coffee, and fruit.*

    *I arrived at the hotel at about 9 a.m. and at 9:30 a.m.
Mr. Anderson called and spent until 2 p.m. with me. He
showed me our new and infant mission here, just 4 years old.
It is interesting. It is in what was a 20-car garage under an*

apartment house. They are having D.V.B.S. this week here. Then we went to Wesley Village where our M.C.O.R. has helped about 80 or 90 refugee families have a home. He told me that we had no work here before the war because Hong Kong is a "Crown Colony" of Britain. By the way it is interesting to see Queen Elizabeth's picture on our dining room wall and British Methodism cared for it. After the war, the refugees from Red China came in such large numbers and some of them were our Methodist Christians and they squatted in terrible shacks on the mountainside. British Methodism asked us to come to help. At Christmas-time in 1953, a terrible fire made homeless 60,000 of these refugees. Methodist Com. on overseas relief started Wesley Village and inspired many other such projects, including government housing. Our work has grown until now we have Wesley Village, two nice churches, and a Christian College, "Chung-Chi."

This afternoon, Mr. Anderson had work, so I took the cable car to the top of the mountain to get a view of the city and harbor. This is a fabulous place. It is a "free port," you know. It is supposed to be a shopper's paradise. I walked through the main shopping streets but did not enjoy it. There are too many people out on the streets spotting "rich Americans" and trying to sell or urge them into their shops.

I went to the Y.M.C.A. for supper and came in early. I had a nice bath, washed all of my Dacron clothes and am about ready for bed. I leave tomorrow at 11:00 a.m. Before going I am to visit our newest church here and then to Calcutta. I must close and try to get some rest. See you in my dreams. Love, Dad

P.S. Glad you will meet me in Chicago. If you think the round trip is too much for one day, and if you can get someone to keep the kids, I don't care if you plan to stay all night up there and get home Sunday. You decide! "Seems strange to be in China."

174

August 31, 1957
Calcutta, India

Dear Folks:

Well, I am just about as far from home as I will ever be. Tonight, I board the airline for Istanbul. Yesterday, I arose early and went to see the people living in shacks on the roof tops in Hong Kong. What a sight!

*At 11:00 a.m. I boarded Cathay in a nice little D.C. 4, a 4-motor, 48 passenger plane at Hong Kong. We came down along the China coast, crossed South Vietnam and Thailand, and landed for one hour at Bangkok. We then came on to Rangoon where we landed for another hour in Burma. Thence we landed in Calcutta by about 1 a.m. according my watch. We lost 3½ hours, so it was only 9:30 p.m. here. I took the bus for downtown after filling out many visa papers. The sights and people are most crowded, dirty, and tragic. The India police are just as inefficient as in Egypt (*ed. note*: where Walter and Emma had visited some years earlier.) You remember how bad that was.*

Through the monsoon rains, I had a good time today and am about ready to leave the airport. Irma Felchlia, a girl from Centralia, showed me around all day and saw me off tonight. She is principal of the Calcutta Christian Girls School, a Women's Society project. I had a nice time seeing her school. The Calcutta Boys School, the Lee Memorial Mission for orphans, the three Methodist churches, Collins Institute, a boy's school sponsored by our Mission Board, plus several sites in the city.

I will try to write you again from either Istanbul or Vienna. Things are going extra well with me. With all my love, Walter

Editor's note: That is the end of the bundled letters from Japan and the Far East. Below is Emma's memory of meeting Walter at the airport in Chicago.

We had to go all the way to Chicago to pick him up at the airport when he came back from Japan. The pastor's wife kept Mark and Debbie. Dave and Kaye and I went to the airport (ed. note: she never mentioned where Buddy was.) Dave thought he had to take care of things, so he took care of all the money and bills to pay on the trip.

Editor's note: Below is a letter from Rev. Nakashima of Oji, Japan that he wrote a few months later to Rev. Martin who was gathering testimonies from people that knew Walter.

January 17, 1958
Oji, Japan

Dear Rev. Martin:

> *I have just received your letter dated the 10th. As here in a local town, it took time to get your letter from Osaka Central Post Office where all of the letters addressed to the area of west of Japan from the foreign countries are collected.*
> *I will go out to the Osaka Central Post Office to mail this letter so that you will be able to get this by the 21st.*
> *First, I tell you the work which we accomplished during the past summer with Rev. Smith. Anyhow, we endeavored to evangelize every day and night. As a result of our effort, God gave us wonderful members. On the last Sunday for Rev. Smith, eight were baptized and three were transferred to our church. This is one of the tokens of the great fruits given to us. We still keep the blessings which he brought.*
> *Second, I tell you the situation of now. After we were given much encouragement by Rev. Smith, we have continued to preach the Gospel and serve God. Then we found the nice place*

to build up our church building. So we contracted to buy the land on the 31st of last month. It costs 555,000 Yen. We have 440,000 Yen which was sent from Dr. Wendell A. Robinson in Carbondale and twenty-five others. We are planning to raise the money for buying the land and for building the church.

We need about 3,000,000 Yen at any rate. As our church members are poor, as Rev. Smith knows, even if we do our best it is impossible to raise all the money. Of course we are going to ask the

Groundbreaking for the Church

churches in Japan to help us. But even so, we will not be able to get enough money.

We need your help to build up our church. We must have a church here in Oji town. We have been grateful to Rev. Smith and all of you for coming to help us last summer. Moreover, we ask you to help us to form the first church.

I don't know whether this letter would make you satisfied or not. But I have told you the truth. We pray for building up our church. And we want you to help us. May God bless all of the churches in your District.

Sincerely yours, Takeshi Nakashima, Pastor of Oji Church.

The Southern Illinois Methodist Bulletin

SOUTHERN ILLINOIS METHODIST, 1960 -- In the summer of 1957, Dr. Walter Smith did missionary work in Japan. He was then District Superintendent of the Olney District. When he returned from Japan he showed pictures in churches and asked the people to help build a new church in Oji Center. The churches responded in the amount of $3,800. The new church was opened for services on December 13th, 1959. The building cost $4,675. The opening service was attended by more than 80 people including the mayor and village alderman who are not Christians. The pastor said, "Everyone was so happy they could not keep from crying. We received five new seekers. I have asked God to help me keep them all coming so that I can catch them. I think our real evangelism starts now." The name of the church has been changed to Nishiyamato Church, which means, "The Church to evangelize the Western half of the province." The pastor is Rev. Takeshi Nakashima and he asks for the prayers of the people of the Olney District who have helped them so much.

###

Clay County Advocate-Press

FLORA, 1958 -- Dr. Walter A. Smith Honored by District Leaders -- Pastors and district leaders of the Olney District of Methodism met Monday night in the Olney First Church for a farewell dinner honoring Dr. Walter A. Smith and family of Flora, who are leaving the community and the work of the district superintendent.

Following the meal, an amateur performance of "This Is Your Life" was presented. This proved most interesting to the group as they looked into Dr. Smith's past and present.

As a look into the future was taken, Dr. D.S. Lacquemont, newly appointed successor to Dr. Smith, appeared on the program.

A gift of silver service was presented to the Smith family, expressing both regret at their leaving and appreciation for consecrated service.

The Smiths will move to Lawrenceville where Dr. Smith will assume duties as pastor of the First Methodist Church. Rev. and Mrs. Lacquemont will move to Flora to begin their work as the leaders of the Olney District.

###

Lawrenceville Daily Record

LAWRENCEVILLE, 1958 -- There will be a covered dish dinner at the First Methodist Church on Wednesday evening, February 12 at 6:30 p.m. in honor of the new preacher, Dr. Walter Smith and family. Please bring your own table service and enough food for your own family. The committee will furnish the drink, only. There will be a program afterwards in the main auditorium. Everyone is invited to attend.

###

Lawrenceville by Emma

On February 1, 1958, the family moved to Lawrenceville, Illinois when Walter was assigned by Bishop Brashares to pastor the First Methodist Church.

One of the ladies in the church was into flowers and flower arranging. She was the Doctor's wife.

The church Committee decided to make the extra space behind the parsonage into a park. Mark said, "They planted a tree on third base," which is where he played ball. This had been the neighborhood playground. It was an act hard for the Smith's to forgive.

Editor's note: This is the point at which Emma stopped writing her family's story. Other people, including her children, completed the family's story.

Lawrenceville by Their Children

We played in the vacant lot behind the parsonage. There were other children in the neighborhood that played with us there. Because it was empty, the lot made for imaginative play for young people, such as a fort made from refrigerator boxes. Only the "king" could enter this fort, but when he was not around, others entered this world of the "Knights of the Round Table."

We played ball in the summer and built snow forts and made snowmen in the winter. We had lots of snowball fights. The youngest of the children always lost these battles. They probably went home crying to their mothers, but we chose not to remember that part of the story.

When the empty lot of a playground was turned into a neighborhood park, we were so disappointed. We could not understand how adults could let this happen to our magical playground. The empty lot had so many happy memories to all of the neighborhood children.

There was a Christmas when one of the youngsters received a new bicycle. The weather was particularly bad that winter and it was many weeks before it was warm enough to ride the new bike outdoors. One warm Sunday morning, the youngster decided to ride the bike outdoors by pretending to be sick and not going to church. Surprisingly, the ploy and play acting worked! After the other family members left for church services the youngster sprang from his "sick bed" and heading outdoors with the new bike.

Apparently the weather was warm enough on that Sunday morning that the church windows were opened. The best sidewalks to ride bikes were next to the church. So up and down the sidewalks went the youngster in gleeful enjoyment all morning, careful to make it back to his "sick bed" before church ended. However, because the church windows were open, everyone in the church that morning heard the sounds of a young child riding his bicycle back and forth throughout the church services, including the horrified parents. The consequences of that day's ride were extreme as the youngster did not see the new bicycle again for a very long time.

The stay in Lawrenceville was not long, as dad was transferred to Fairfield.

Wayne County Press

FAIRFIELD, June 30, 1960 -- SURROUNDED! You can hardly see City Councilman Arthur Craig (rear, with hat) and the Rev. Walter A. Smith (beside Craig to his left), new pastor of the First Methodist Church, who are surrounded by a few youthful ball players who participated in Saturday's tag day.

Fairfield by Their Children

In 1960 the family moved to Fairfield and lived in the parsonage on Delaware street. The parsonage had two stories with two bedrooms upstairs and three down. Dave had his own and Buddy and Mark shared the second upstairs. There were two bedrooms downstairs with a bathroom connecting them. Kaye had one of the bedrooms and dad and mom the other. A utility room was converted into a bedroom for Debbie.

From a railing on a balcony on the second floor ran a stairwell to the main floor and a basement, with switchbacks connecting each level. There were porches in front on two sides and a small, fenced-in backyard where ball games were played.

The grade and high school buildings were within easy walking distance, although the building for kindergarten and first grade was a bus ride away. Debbie admitted that she often hid from the bus when it came in the mornings, but must not have hidden very well as the driver would honk until she relented and boarded the bus for school. She's not sure if she was just being a brat or if there was some sort of trauma associated with busing to that school, but she didn't want to go there.

Buddy admitted he often sneaked out of his second story bedroom window and went down the TV antenna. He got a spanking from dad, which he admitted he deserved. He thought he was a bad influence with the neighbor kids. He once built electronic "walkie-talkies" with his friend Dennis Lofton, but they worked poorly. Yelling reached the other person farther than the electronic devices they built.

We mostly played on the grade school's playground about a block away. It had swings, teeter-totters, sidewalks for playing hop-scotch, and much more. Sometimes we played in our backyard. It was not large, but was big enough for whiffle ball and running games. There was a carport with a shed attached that seemed to me to be very high. Buddy liked to climb on top of it and jump to the ground. When he urged the smaller ones to climb up top with him, we refused, probably crying and running to our mother.

The boys had an electric toy train with the track mounted on a sheet of plywood. The older kids would drop aspirin-sized tablets into the smokestack of the train's engine and "smoke" would billow out of it as the train traveled around on the track. The flipside of the sheet of plywood was painted and we would attach a net to it and play ping-pong.

Other Places Where We Have Lived
By Emma & Others

Buddy kept a hamster in a cage in the basement. At least once the hamster found a way to get out of its cage at night and climb the stairs all the way from the basement to the second story where it was found the next morning in bed with Buddy.

The Petersons lived in the house behind us in a very large house, three stories high if remembered correctly. Their backyard was large with trees and room to run. They had several children that were similar in age to us. We would climb in their trees. Kaye may have fallen out of their tree and broken her arm. Buddy would hide in their tree and throw acorns at passersby. In the back of their house was an old shed; probably used to house horses during an era before cars were prevalent. It had a small loft where we could hide away.

The Johnsons lived next door and across the side street. They tore down their house when they moved. Mr. Johnson owned a gas station a few houses away. It was called East Side Garage, but was on the west side of town. The Loftins were good friends and we played lots of ping pong at their house almost every night after school. There was a go cart we drove in the streets. Later we bought a moped.

We continued to take camping trips to national parks, state parks, and many other places of interest. We outgrew the small trailer we owned, so our parents bought a larger one that was a little more accommodating to their growing family. If remembered correctly, Dave and Buddy slept in a pup tent, Mark slept on the floor of the trailer, Deb slept in an overhead bunk bed, and Kaye slept in a bed that was converted from the kitchen table area.

The Methodist Church in Fairfield was a familiar old style brick structure with a square bell tower. It had a basement where we roamed while waiting for our parents after meetings and services. We used to tease mom about having to turn out all the lights before we could go home. Dad often left early and worked late, after the bedtime for small children. Mom would have the younger ones take afternoon naps so that they could stay up late to see dad when he got home. She would make us peanut butter and jelly sandwiches for our late night snacks.

While in Fairfield, dad helped the church add an educational wing onto the lovely church building. Dad was an integral part in church's expansion. We were so impressed with the silver painted shovels the men held during the ground breaking ceremony. As small children, we watched the progress of the building each Sunday morning as we attended church. Finally it was built and we attended our first Sunday school classes in the new educational wing. The building smelled new and everyone seemed so excited. The newness wore off, but the excitement at the time still remains a wonderful memory for a youngster.

The Southern Illinois Methodist Bulletin

FAIRFIELD, August 1961 -- Sunday June 11, 1961 was a day to be remembered at the First Methodist Church of Fairfield, Ill. After more than three years of planning and fund raising, ground was broken for a new educational building.

A small area was roped off on the west side of the church. In the center of this area a cross was formed on the ground with powdered lime. At the close of the ritual consecration of the ground, each of the ten officials in the church turned a spadeful (sic) of earth.

First to break the ground was the new Superintendent of the Harrisburg District, Dr. Clyde Funkhouser. There followed in turn the pastor, the chairman of the Building Committee, the chairman of the Official Board, the Church School Superintendent, the chairman of the Commission on Education, the president of the Methodist Men, the President of the WSCS, the president of MYF, and a child chosen by the junior department of the church school.

The ribbon bedecked shovel, with a shiny new coat of silver paint, was the one that Rev. Smith used in a number of services of this kind during six years as the Olney District Superintendent.

The $160,000 project to build fourteen new class rooms, some office space, and renovate the present building is expected to proceed promptly and to be completed about Christmas this year.

###

On the Beat by Cub Reporter Tom Mathew, Jr. -- Wayne County Press

FAIRFIELD, undated -- The singing sounded pretty at the Methodist church Sunday morning. Almost better than usual! Why? There was an all male choir with the Cub singing basso profundo (ed. note: "Cub" is the name Mathews called himself and is used to designate an inexperienced reporter.) It is fun to sing in the choir ... you can see who's taking a nap during the sermon.

The preaching was tops, too. It was Layman's Sunday and Dr. Walter Smith was on the sideline while Ken Ward, Dick Hoard, Dick Cochran, and Joe Fleming carried the ball. Fine job men!

###

Wayne County Press

FAIRFIELD, 1963 -- Fairfield First Methodist church is losing its pastor, Dr. Walter A. Smith. Pastor here since 1960, Dr. Smith on Monday was named new Executive Secretary of the Southern Illinois Conference of the Methodist Church.

Dr. Smith, whose appointment was announced by Bishop Edwin Edgar Voight, will assume his new duties June 1st, and will reside in Mt. Vernon, where he will establish his headquarters.

He has been a minister in the conference 25 years, coming to Fairfield from Lawrenceville.

The position of executive director was created by a special session of the Southern Illinois Annual Conference February 14th, when the conference also voted to employ a lay associate secretary. The two positions represent consolidation of five existing offices. Bishop Voigt is expected to appoint the lay associate soon.

In his new post, Dr. Smith will be responsible to the conference cabinet for the development and coordination of programs and activities of 462 Methodist churches in 39 counties in the lower one-third of

Illinois. The conference beginning June 1ˢᵗ will be divided into five districts with a total of 252 charges, an estimated 79,730 members and an aggregate budget of $4,381,780.

Dr. Smith, a native of Alto Pass, has degrees from Southern Illinois University and the University of Illinois and in 1946 obtained a B.D. degree from Garret Biblical Institute at Evanston.

He has served as superintendent of the Olney district in addition to various church pastorates. He is married to the former Emma L. Lutes of Christopher and they have five children.

While in Fairfield, Dr. Smith has served as a member of the Community Development Committee. He has been chairman of the conference board of ministerial training and is a former dean of the Illinois College of Christian Life.

Dr. Smith's new post will bring appointment of a new pastor to the Fairfield church.

In commenting about leaving Fairfield, Dr. Smith said, "My family and I have enjoyed living in Fairfield and we regret leaving. We have enjoyed splendid cooperation from church members in our work here for which we are deeply grateful."

"The new assignment," he continued, "presents a genuine challenge for us in the months ahead."

While he was in Fairfield, Dr. Smith guided his church in the construction of a new $150,000 educational building completed last spring.

###

On the Beat by Cub Reporter Tom Mathew, Jr. -- Wayne County Press

FAIRFIELD, 1963 -- A warm welcome to Dr. Delbert Lacquement (sic) as a new member of the clergy of our city. The family will be valuable additions to our community and we wish them a long and fruitful ministry at the First Methodist Church.

Now that he's gone and won't be seeing what we write, I reckon it'll be safe to say a few things about the Methodist preacher who just left town. We refer to Dr. Walter A. Smith.

He was different than any Methodist minister we ever knew. You'll find one or two of his "rare" characteristics in nearly every preacher that comes along, but seldom will you find all of them in one package. But he had them all.

He was as common and ordinary as an old shoe. He dressed modestly ... seldom wore a robe in church, we wished he had worn one more, and he carried with him not the slightest tinge of "salve" or "put-on." Though his manner was meek and mild and his stature small, he reminded us of a little general and his tongue was sharper than a razor's edge when he saw a need to cut someone down.

We've heard him do a beautiful job of "trimming up" faithful choir members who'd slip out of church following the anthem. We've heard him dress down "pillars" of the church for walking out before the benediction. One time he said, "If you people ever find a perfect church don't go to it because you'd spoil it for sure!"

He didn't go in for a lot of fanfare at Eastertime (sic) and he was ice cold about lavish decorations at Christmas. He'd pick hymns that were unfamiliar and hard to sing and somewhere along the line it seems that we heard church members screaming because he failed to make the janitor ring the church bell on Sunday morning. But with it all, he held the love and admiration of his congregation and he demonstrated more self-confidence than any preacher we ever knew. Why do we say this? Because he twisted around the order of church worship to the point that he had the ushers taking up offerings following his sermon. Who ever heard of that? In most churches you pay before you listen but not so with Walter Smith. First, he let 'em see what he had to offer and then pay if they wanted to ... and they always did. All in all he was a great person and we wish him success in his new assignment.

Now, we'll rise for the benediction and I'll see you all next week. So long!

###

Mt. Vernon Register News

MT. VERNON, 1964 -- The Methodist Church in Southern Illinois yesterday, in Mt. Vernon, outlined its program for 1964-65, including unconventional evangelism "where the people are," a proposal to establish an inter-racial congregation, and suggested expenditures of $147,700 in support of Christian higher education.

Coordinating Council of Southern Illinois Conference, meeting in Mt. Vernon, applauded the comment of Dr. Walter Smith, executive secretary that "the church cannot stand still in an age like this."

Bishop Edwin E. Voigt, Springfield, led the session from which development boards and agencies' plans (were) to be presented for approval by annual meeting of the Conference in May.

Plans submitted yesterday are, perhaps, the most far-reaching attempts in recent history to extend the witness of the church into every home and community.

The annual session in May will be asked to approve preaching services in such unconventional places as state fairs, county fairs, state parks, in tent revivals, and over coffee cups.

At the same time, local pastors will be summoned to join "Operation Recovery," to return inactive members to active membership.

Some of the most dramatic Christian expression is expected to emerge from plans of the board of Christian social concerns to effect (sic) a closer relationship between white and Negro sections of local Methodism. In keeping with a gathering concern of the Methodist church to divorce itself from the label of segregated congregations, Southern Illinois Conference will explore closely ways and means to establish an inter-racial congregation. Spokesmen for the plan declined to comment on location of the new group, however.

A second emphasis of the board would be stepped up education of Methodists on the evils of gambling.

###

Mt. Vernon by Their Children

After three years in Fairfield, dad was appointed as the first Executive Secretary of the newly formed Coordinating Council of Southern Illinois Conference in 1963, now called the Council of Ministry. Charlie remembered that they often helped dad clean his "office" on Friday evenings.

Our first house was at the end of Simpson Drive. It was on a street, down in a gulley that is now a wonderful subdivision. Back then there were many undeveloped places to explore; densely wooded areas, creek beds, railroad tracks, and a newly developed neighborhood in back of the house, just up the hill and across the creek in another highly wooded area.

We would often explore the partially built houses in the new development behind our house. On one occasion mom stepped on a nail and was laid up for a while. We all learned to watch our step around new construction, or that maybe we shouldn't be so nosey about other people's property.

Behind the house was a drainage type creek that came from a pond up the hill. Mark and Debbie would dig into the banks of the dry creek making roads and houses for his Matchbox cars. In winter we would spend hours skating on the pond up the hill when it was adequately frozen over.

Sometimes on Saturday night dad would bring home a sack of Reban's hamburgers, seven for $1.00. What a deal! When the older kids were home it was just enough sandwiches for the entire crew. Another weekend treat was root beer floats and popcorn.

Several times, in the evenings, we helped out at dad's office by stuffing letters into envelopes. While we lived in the house on Simpson Drive, Debbie took piano lessons and remembers practicing on the piano in the front room begrudgingly. She also remembers "waltzing" with dad in that same front room. He loved music and once said to her that he thought the early Beatles songs had pretty good lyrics. Charlie got his amateur radio operators license and would talk to strangers for hours. He belonged to the high school radio club.

Each year dad would order a new Christmas music album put out by Firestone. Dad had records by artists like Andy Williams, Johnny Mathis, Philadelphia Orchestra, and many others. One of our favorites was *The Grand Canyon Suite*. It was quite dramatic because the orchestra music was made to sound like a storm over the Grand Canyon.

A couple of years in early December we would take a shopping trip to St. Louis to see the decorated windows of Famous Barr for the holiday season. In the summer we went to the open air stage of the St. Louis Municipal Opera. The performance remembered best was *The King and I* with Roberta Peters and James Shigeta.

Railroad tracks, not far into the woods nearby, led to the hospital grounds and a large field where kids in that part of town could play all sorts of games. Soccer and football were my favorites. The kids living near there had a basketball goal at their house that attracted many of us on cool fall evenings. Hank Woolsey was a good friend. There was a vacant lot behind his house where we played homerun derby with whiffle balls and bats.

Weather permitting we walked or rode our bikes to school, which seemed like a big deal at the time. When the weather was bad we were dropped off and picked up by our parents. As an older child at the grade school, Mark volunteered to be a crossing guard that helped the younger students across busy streets. His parents were thrilled that he took

Emma & her "Gray Ladies" Uniform, 2016

responsibility of the younger ones. He liked the volunteer job because he got out of class a few minutes early each day to wait for the younger children to be dismissed from school and come his way. His parents were never told that he was allowed to leave class early to do this job. He figured it was a need to know situation and they didn't need to know.

Behind the Mt. Vernon Good Samaritan Hospital in the 1960s was a Tuberculosis Sanatorium. Before the discovery and wide use of antibiotics that controlled and virtually eliminated TB, people who contracted tuberculosis were segregated to prevent the spread of this highly contagious disease. Emma volunteered in the TB Sanatorium as a "Gray Lady," named for the gray colored Red Cross uniforms worn. She spent hours talking to patients with TB, writing letters for them, and buying personal items that they requested from town. The Mt. Vernon TB Sanatorium opened in 1951 and closed in 1974.

John Mark (as he was called then) played basketball from the sixth through the eighth grade. Dad came to many of his games. He was a proud papa. We played baseball in Little League in the summer and our parents came when they could. With such a large family and many church responsibilities, they didn't always have the time. They were not like today's parents that attend all of the games their children played. We were okay with that.

Dad stopped working for the conference and we moved to a new house on Southwest Crescent Drive in 1968. It was a split level house. We lived there only a short time before a tornado hit our house while we were away on a camping trip. A park ranger notified us about midnight that we had storm damage. At first our parents decided to wait until daybreak to go back home, but since neither could sleep they decided to pack up and leave in the middle of the night. We packed up and traveled home to find police lights and barricades to the entrance to our street. After confirming our identity we were allowed to pass to see spotlights on what was left of our house.

When we got to Mt. Vernon we could see that the top part of our house was gone. Some of the walls of the main floor were left standing, the rest was gone. The piano that Debbie begrudgingly learned to play was boldly still there sitting upright, exposed to the elements -- rain and sun. What remained was drenched in

Tornado's Destruction, 1968

the rain that followed. Virtually all of our belongings were gone or ruined by rain and insulation from the attic. We wanted to save a few of our favorite items, but most of it was turned over to our insurance company for reimbursement.

Editor's note: In a letter from former neighbors Kerry, Kim and Kirk Pace, they said the following about the tornado and our house.

"We came to love all the Smiths and especially to appreciate Emma's dry humor. Never was this humor as evident as on the occasion of a tornado in Mt. Vernon. The tornado came just after the Smiths moved into their brand new, first home on Crescent Drive. When the Mt. Vernon radio reported that Country Heights had been especially hard hit, we called to inquire about the Smiths and their house. Emma, in her matter-of-fact voice and what we thought to be dry humor, said, 'We are all right (sic) but our roof is over in our neighbor's back yard!' We said, 'No, really, did you have any damage?' Emma replied, 'Yes, our roof is really in our neighbor's yard, our living room and piano open to the sky and rain.' Emma's voice somehow remained calm and all the Smiths calm, collected and very flexible."

While our house was being rebuilt, we moved into an apartment on an upper floor of the Emerson Hotel in downtown Mt. Vernon. John Mark slept in the living room/kitchen area of the apartment and Debbie slept on a roll away bed in the bedroom with dad and mom. Later, after graduating from college, Charlie (as he was called by the family at this time) moved in with us and he and John Mark shared a second hotel room.

While living in the hotel, we watched the moon landing, listened to Beatles music, and watched pigeons outside of the windows. John Mark walked to high school a few blocks away.

After dad left as Executive Secretary of the Methodist Church he taught school for a year at Casey Junior High School during Debbie's final year there, from the fall of 1969 to the spring of 1970. One subject he taught was a math class. A couple of girls from the class ganged up on Debbie and insisted that dad make their grade an "A" in math. There was another incident or two that involved kids bullying her. Dad had enough of teaching youngsters and after Debbie graduated from junior high school and John Mark from high school he sought other employment. He never taught in public schools again after that one year at the junior high.

In the fall of 1969 mom taught second grade at Woodlawn Elementary School. She taught 28 students. She told us later that our cousin Peggy O'Daniell was hired to take her place when she resigned in 1970.

We left Mt. Vernon in 1970 after living there for seven years, which was actually our longest time in any town until then.

Mt. Vernon Register News

MT. VERNON, July 15, 1970 -- The Rev. Walter A. Smith has been employed as Director of Admissions at McKendree College, Lebanon, Illinois, according to an announcement by President Eric N. Rackham.

A graduate of Southern Illinois University, he received his master's degree from University of Illinois and received his B.D. degree (Baccalaureate in Divinity in 1946) from Garret (sic) Theological Seminary. In 1954, he was awarded the D.D. degree (Doctor of Divinity) from McKendree College.

For the past six years Mr. Smith was Director of Programs for the Southern Illinois Conference, with his office located in Mt. Vernon. This past year he taught in the Mt. Vernon public schools.

He will visit high schools and junior college campuses to advise the guidance personnel and students who want assistance regarding plans and possibilities for higher education.

He is married to the former Emma L. Lutes. They reside at 420 Parkview Drive, Lebanon, Illinois. They are the parents of five children: Kaye married to Terry Kimpling; David, a graduate of SIU who is in the armed services and due to be released soon; Charles, a graduate of SIU and a positioning engineer for the State Highway Department; John, a freshman at McKendree College; and Deb, a freshman at Lebanon Community High School.

###

Lebanon by Their Children

Dad was hired as the Director of Admissions for McKendree College in Lebanon in 1970. The school was renamed McKendree University decades later. We moved to Lebanon and into a small ranch style house with a brick front.

John was dad's first recruit. Instead of attending Southern Illinois University as had been planned, his parents asked that he go to McKendree instead so that dad could get his recruiting career off to a good start. John was reluctant at first, but after an on campus visit he agreed to attend McKendree as dad's first official recruit. His parents were both very proud that he changed his college plans to help them get off to a good start at McKendree.

Many of Deb's friends were children of the military at nearby Scott Air Force Base, so many of them moved in and out of her life.

Camping was still a part of family vacations. Dad and mom had sold the little Comet camper before leaving Mt. Vernon and purchased a larger Layton brand camper. Dad experimented with different hitches and spring and shock setups, none that he felt very confident to travel with. We camped and traveled less and less using the Layton camper so it was sold.

McKendree College was very small, about 500 students back then. Mt. Vernon High School had 1,700 students, so it was an adjustment for John. Classes, especially the math and science classes had only a handful of students. The Chemistry class had only three. After living at home the first year, John lived on campus for his sophomore year helping him learn more about "college life." He still wasn't far from home and his parents kept close tabs. Dad knew that McKendree College and living in Lebanon was difficult on a young man trying to understand his place in the world. Wanting a bigger and more distant college experience was inevitable. Dad allowed and encouraged John to transfer to Illinois State University in Normal for his final two years of college.

Two days after graduating high school, Deb moved to Effingham to live with her sister Kaye, her husband Terry, and their daughter Bonnie. After a couple of months she began working at a factory and found her own place to live.

The family left Lebanon after the youngest, Deb, graduated from high school.

Albion Journal Register

ALBION, 1974 -- Rev. Walter Smith, a former District Supt. of the Olney District, is the new minister of the First United Methodist Church. The pastor and wife, Emma, moved into the parsonage Thursday. He succeeds Rev. Sam Totten, who was assigned to Fairview Heights.

###

Albion by Their Children

After four years in Lebanon, dad accepted a charge with the First Methodist Church in Albion in 1974. Their children were away from home by then, but visited them in Albion as often as they could. It seemed like a nice little town and church. Mom entered several items at the Edwards County Fair and won many first, second, and third premium ribbons, one ribbon was for her famous Begonia flowers. She also entered a knot-weaving wall display item made by one of her children, which won a blue, first premium ribbon. We still have the blue ribbon.

Many of Walter's Sunday sermons were recorded by Emma in the Albion First United Methodist Church. These cassette recordings were captured on digital media many years later by their children.

After a couple of years in Albion, they were transferred to Anna, Illinois by the Methodist Conference.

Anna by Their Children

Dad transferred to the First United Methodist Church in Anna, just a few miles south of where the couple first started their ministry for churches in and around Makanda. While in Anna, dad was successful in getting the church to agree to buy a new parsonage. The old one, we were told, was not suitable for the next pastor if he had a family. Mom continued to enter crafts in the County Fair in Anna and again won many first, second, and third premium awards. They made wonderful, lasting friends in Anna.

Carbondale by Their Children

While still living in Anna, our parents bought a house in Carbondale on Rod Lane. It had three bedrooms and a full, unfinished basement. Throughout the months before dad's retirement, they often came to Carbondale from their charge in Anna to paint and otherwise fix up their new homestead for their eventual move there soon after his retirement in 1978.

They spent twenty wonderful years together in Carbondale before dad's passing in 1998. They rediscovered travel to exotic places during those twenty years, but mostly travelled with tour groups, such as Five Star Tours that was associated with John's work with the senior citizens center in Herrin.

A neighbor's dog was housed just outside of mom's kitchen window. It was a very large dog that would bark very loudly and incessantly at any sight of movement, both animal and human including mom. One afternoon mom whispered to the dog for a rather long period of time. We could not hear what was said, but after that encounter the dog never barked when it saw mom approach, unlike other people or animals within its eyesight.

Dad took several classes at John A. Logan College in small engine repair learning to repair lawn mower engines. He was quite good at repairs and used his skill on his and his children's mowers. He also pursued clock repairs after he took correspondence classes and learned enough to start a small business repairing grandfather and mantle clocks for his family, friends, and a few people who contacted him. He advertised his business as "The Clock Doc."

Occasionally, dad would serve as a substitute minister in churches that needed someone to preach for a Sunday or two. Later, mom said that the anxiety of preaching before strangers was too much for him, so he stopped.

For many years, mom was very active in the United Methodist Women's group, serving as their President during the time when the Southern and Central Illinois conferences became united as one. She helped with coordination activities during the unification period.

Mom spent many hours with arts and crafts; making pottery, knitting, crocheting, and making many craft-related gifts for her family at Christmastime.

SIU Class Reunion of 1939 -- October 20, 1989

Editor's note: The following is from an invitation for the 50th reunion of the Southern Illinois University graduating class of 1939. Later, Walter wrote of his memories as a student commuting to SIU and his graduation in 1939.

> *Dear Classmates,*
>
> *The Class of 1939 was inducted into Southern Illinois State Normal University in September 1935, by Roscoe Pulliam. In the fourth year of his presidency, Mr. Pulliam signed our diplomas and, at the request of the class members, spoke at our Commencement exercises on June 2, 1939. The theme of our 50th class reunion is to be "A Salute to the Roscoe Pulliam Presidency."*
>
> *You are encouraged to begin planning for this 1989 Homecoming weekend of activities. We hope you will be able to attend the reception and dinner meeting which will highlight the reunion of the Class of '39 and our induction into the Half Century Club of the Southern Illinois University Alumni Association of Friday evening, October 20, in the Student Center.*

Attached is the '39 class roster with the latest addresses which the Alumni Office has obtained. Your first assignment is to help locate classmates for whom incomplete information is on file. Second, your support of the SIU Alumni Association is solicited. A special senior citizen membership rate is available to you. You are also requested to send an up-to-date biography of 150-200 words for inclusion in the special publication being developed for this reunion.

Class President Winston McAdoo of Dorien, Connecticut, is making plans to participate in this reunion. Mrs. Mabel Pulliam Sattgast, at age 90, is looking forward to seeing you. Bob Pulliam is preparing a special article about his father for the class brochure. Willard Kerr, Herbert Johnson, Marie Williams, David Aiken, Martha Jean Langenfeld Rasche, George Boomer, Harland Cade, Gaylord Whitlock, and Bonnie Favrot Allen are among those who are supportive of the class tribute to Mr. Pulliam. Perhaps a class reunion gift can materialize to support the Roscoe Pulliam Scholarship Fund for meritorious and needy students planning to attend SIUC.

We are aware of the problems of health, distance, and conflicts with your other responsibilities which may prevent some of you from attending; however, we want your support for this reunion. You will receive the program brochure and a report on the event even though you cannot attend. Most importantly, we want you and your spouse or friend to attend this reunion and to visit with your classmates of 50 years ago.

The Southern Illinoisan Newspaper

CARBONDALE, August 1991 -- The Rev. and Mrs. Walter A. Smith of Carbondale will celebrate their 50th wedding anniversary from 2 to 4 pm on August 4, 1991 at the Carbondale United Methodist Church.

Smith and Emma Lutes were married in August 1941 in Makanda. Smith is a retired Methodist minister.

The couple have five children, David Smith of Raleigh, N.C., Kaye Kimpling, Debbie Gregory and Charles Smith all of Effingham, and John Smith of Carbondale. They also have four grandchildren.

The children of the couple request friends of the family submit old pictures, write down memories, or send cards for a scrapbook to Kaye Kimpling ... Friends and relatives are invited to attend.

1991 Letter by Others

Dear Walter and Emma,

My, we go back a long way, don't we? Can it really be half a century? My first meeting was in my beloved little country church, Zion, on the Makanda charge. I remember a brisk young preacher boy with crisp curly black hair and earnest intense black eyes. He played a guitar and sang "There's an All-Seeing Eye Watching You" among other things.

He was always welcome at Roy and Gussie's table and I, like many other girls with young preachers, got a mild crush on the new parson. I remember I was still interested enough to appreciate the irony when Emma was in a rush and borrowed a dollar from me to have her hair "done" for their first date. It must have been love at first sight for they were definitely a "thing" from that time on. I remember the wedding -- sweet and tender and obviously lasting. Not many can say they've seen their preacher ridden on a rail or helped give the newlyweds a pounding.

After Bill and I found each other, we wanted Walter to perform the ceremony -- he tied a lasting knot, too. I've always felt that we were friends, isn't that enough? The years have spun faster than this vehicle spins 'round the track and inconceivably we're retired and find that somehow in that half-century we've grown from eager young people to not-so-young people who I hope are still eager about the affairs of the heart and the affairs of the world. As I said, the word "friend" is enough.

###

Editor's note: the following combines several documents into one letter.

Tributes from Their Children

Dear Mom and Dad,

There is not just one single memory that stands out, but snippets of events that stand out from our childhood. Some of our memories over the years in which we've been a part with you involve the many camping and travelling trips we took as a family. You always made sure we got to see and appreciate so many of the natural wonders of our country -- the Grand Canyon which is sure "grand alright"; the "Johnson Shut-outs, uh, Shut-ins, oh shut-up; Glacier National Park with the long hike up the glacier which seemed like such a good way to get there until about half-way up and us in slick, leather sole shoes that kept sliding toward the crevice, we were sure glad to see dad's arm to hang on to!; driving around and round San Francisco looking for the TV studio that was in L.A.; Turkey Run before the waterslide; Niagara Falls; and so many other neat places and good times. We would play games in the car ride to help the long miles go by a little faster. In the afternoons we might find a Dairy Queen to stop at to take a break and buy some ice cream. Thanks for these memories and so many more.

When we were children and dad came home late from work, mom might wake us up to spend a few minutes with dad before we went back to bed. When we visited grandma

*and granddad Smith in the country or on their farm, we
would have fun places to play. We loved watching the cows
and hated stepping in
the "cow piles!" We
soon learned to watch
were we walked. At
Christmastime we
would go to Famous
Barr in St. Louis and
park in the big garage*

The Smith Family, 1991

*across the street. Looking at the Christmas decorations and
running up and down the escalators was fun. Easter was
great because we all got special Easter clothes or hats to wear
and hoped it was warm enough to wear them.*

*Thanks also for giving us a solid foundation built on sound
Christian principals from which we have been able to grow and
find our own happiness. It was such a luxury to have mom
stay at home with us kids while we were little. Your examples
of living your beliefs, concern for others, and love of one another
were standards for us all to reach for.*

*Most of all, you were blessed with 50 years together and
have truly made the most of them!*

Thanks for the love and the memories. We love you both.

###

50<u>th</u> Class Reunion of Garrett Seminary in 1996

<u>Editor's note</u>: The following was written in May 1996 by Walter to
Garrett-Evangelical Theological Seminary as a brief biographical sketch
of his appointments and churches served since graduating from Garrett.
This profile was written in anticipation of his 50th anniversary and the
reunion with his graduating class of 1946.

Upon leaving Garrett, Emma and I decided to return to our home Conference in Southern Illinois. We were appointed to a nice little congregation in the village of Equality, what a nice name. We found there loving, caring church families that was easy to call home.

After just three years we were moved to the First Methodist Church in Olney where we found a congregation of about 1,000 members. It was a big change for us, but the training that Garrett gave made us better prepared for the challenge. In Olney everything we tried worked well and we had four fruitful years. An example, we had five young men enter the ministry, four of whom returned to the Southern Illinois Conference.

Next, after four years, the Bishop appointed me as District Superintendent of the Olney District. I was just seven years out of Seminary, and served as the youngest District Superintendent in the North Central Jurisdiction of our church. Though difficult for Emma and our young family, five children, I thoroughly enjoyed these six years of ministry.

Following the Superintendency, we served pastorates in two of our finest Southern Illinois churches, Lawrence and Fairfield.

In 1963, our Conference formed what we now call a Council on Ministry and I was appointed as our first Executive Director. For six years I travelled all over our Conference trying to help the local churches get a broad vision of the new ministry in Christian education, global and local missions, Christian Social Concerns, etc. These years were very gratifying and meaningful.

My next appointment was as Director of Admissions at McKendree College in Lebanon, Illinois. Working with Senior High and college students gave me great satisfaction. After just four years, back to the pastorate we went.

We completed 40 years of ministry to the Sunday (ed. note: he probably meant "the Church") *and retired. It was a great journey into which I had poured my energies. My only regret is that I didn't relay more and enjoy my family more. Yet, our children are doing well. They love the church and their parents. What more could one ask!*

My Conference gave me many honors. I served on almost every Board and Committee. I was chairperson of the Conference Board of the Ordained Ministry as it is now called. Twice my Conference sent me as a delegate to General Conference and four times to the North Central Jurisdictional Conference as a delegate.

As I approached retirement I realized that I did not have a hobby. So, having had a long time interest in clocks, I took a correspondence course in clock repair. Since there are many old clocks treasured as family looms, I make a lot of friends by repairing their old clocks. This occupies a lot of my time and gives me a chance to witness to God's goodness in granting us time. Thus the journey continues, filled with joy.

Walter A. Smith

Winters Spent in Florida by Emma

Walter & the Camper in Florida

Walter's mother and father had been traveling each winter to Avon Park Holiness Church Camp in Avon Park, Florida. After Walter's father passed away Walter's mother still wanted to go to the church camp. We drove her down and stayed during the ten-day Camp Meeting.

We decided we really liked it there. Rather than spending only ten days during camp meeting period we decided to stay the entire winter in Avon Park. Walter wanted to avoid the possibility of driving to Florida in inclement weather, so the Smith family began the tradition of celebrating Christmas together on the Friday after Thanksgiving.

We left a week or so after the family celebration to travel to Florida for the winter. We returned each year to Avon Park for more than twenty years together.

At first we stayed in Schoenhal dorm on the 4th floor. There wasn't any air-conditioning. We found that leaving a window open on the east and west ends allowed night breezes to go through.

While driving around on a day trip during the second winter, we saw a camper for sale. We met with the seller and agreed on a price. After we purchased it, the seller moved the camper into Avon Park Holiness Camp for us. We had a carport built onto it and stayed in the camper for many winters. During the camp meeting period Walter would volunteer to make the coffee and I would wait tables. Walter enjoyed shuffle board and every afternoon he and several other men would play. I enjoyed crafting with the other women. We would drive often with friends several times each winter to watch spring training baseball games. We made many friends and had a wonderful experience wintering in Florida.

In the fall of 1997 Walter had a stroke and we decided to stay in Illinois that winter. We made the decision to sell our camper in Florida. The man who bought it was from the Granite City area. Walter affectionately called him "The Kid" and we all became good friends. Walter passed in January 1998 on my birthday.

The following fall I felt strong enough to return to Holiness camp in Avon Park. My five children took turns driving me in my car down there and then flying back home each winter. In the spring they took turns again, flying down to Florida and driving my car home to Illinois. This allowed me to have my own transportation while in Florida. I rented a lady's camper for two winters until an apartment came up for sponsorship.

I went to Florida solo for almost twenty more years. At age 92 my children convinced me that I should no longer drive and so I sold my car. Afterwards my children took turns transporting me to Florida in their vehicles. After I gave up driving, my oldest child Dave bought a second home in Avon Park. Dave drove me to church, grocery shopping and generally kept an eye on me while in Florida. Friends at the camp would take me on day trips and shopping adventures.

Editor's note: Also remembered from time in spent Florida are the country store by the orange grove that served orange ice cream -- a family favorite, the Methodist Church in Avon Park that we attended, Bok Tower especially on Easter Sunday, Highlands State Park and its crocodiles or were they alligators, Lake Isis near the campground, the town that painted murals on the sides of its buildings, beautiful flowers in the winter, and the nice people in the camp.

Eating Orange Ice Cream
at the Country Store

Editor's note: The following is edited from a journal of notes written by Emma. A few editorial changes were made to clarify some of the events.

Walter's Illness and Widowhood by Emma

Dear Journal:

On November 10, 1997 at 7:30 pm Walt had a stroke. He had been having symptoms but we thought it was the flu. That night he complained that he didn't feel well, clutched his left eye, and said his head was "breaking out." Later he couldn't verbalize any words and went to bed. He slept fitfully with the bedroom light left on.

When we awoke the next morning Walt still couldn't say any words. We called the doctor and saw him later that day. The doctor gave him a thorough exam, said his blood pressure was 124 over 70, and set up further tests. Walt slept most of the day, was in and out of consciousness throughout, and seemed cold. The next few weeks were filled with medical exams, good improvement in motor skills but slower advancement in his verbal and writing skills even with therapy and practice with my encouragement. The doctors' reports were all very encouraging.

Walt helped with the household chores, laundry, vacuuming, and assisted with the shopping. He would pay for the groceries with dollars bills but had trouble with the change. He told me when to write the checks to pay bills and how he balanced the checkbook, but he had trouble with the numbers. He had trouble telling time except for the hour and half hour.

The Wednesday before Thanksgiving he was asked at therapy about family. He burst out crying. Later he told me he was frustrated and mad that he had his stroke just when the traditional family gathering was to take place and when we were to go to Florida for the winter. Upon consideration, he decided he was thankful that the stroke happened at home on not on the way to or in Florida.

John came by our house on Thanksgiving Day and that seemed to help his mood some. We watched the Macy's Parade together. It went by too fast with too much information for him to follow it closely, which made him sick. I questioned him at length about going to the family gathering the next day. He didn't feel he could physically go. We took a drive and he broke out in song for the first time since the stroke.

The Friday after Thanksgiving he was mad because he couldn't go to Effingham for the family gathering. When the family called us he had trouble determining who was talking and what they were saying. It all went too swiftly for him to comprehend.

He worried about a bill that came from in the mail from the Florida power company. It was a routine power bill we get when the camp is open. He worried about everything. We went for a ride, at his wish, to Murphysboro, DeSoto and then home. Around 8 pm, Dave came to spend the night. Walt was ready for bed but perked up and visited with Dave until 10 pm. Walt slept well and slept late the next day.

The next day, Dave stayed until after lunch. We went to the Mall and walked then bought milk and came home. Walt wound the clocks and I went after the newspaper. It was the first time I had left him alone at home. Bill and Normagene visited us later that day. Walt worried about the camper in Florida -- was the refrigerator door open, who would plug it in, etc. We decided to sell the camper as it was too much for us to deal with.

Therapy went well -- he was using compound words but making choices was difficult. Choices were easier if they were multiple choices and he could see the answers. We spent mornings writing, he writes in his daily "suggester," a homework assignment from therapy. It is hard but he is determined.

I hated making him do the piddling therapy work as it is so demeaning but necessary. He often seems depressed about it. I asked him to go over his assignment and hated that it got harder. We tried to memorize it instead of thinking it through. We went through the house and I had him name the household objects. He did his assignment one more time and it was easier.

We need mornings to rest before going to therapy. He didn't do so well with either assignment or naming objects at therapy. It makes him sick to his stomach as he tries so hard. His retention and phonics need more work.

We walked at the Mall and received many phone calls from friends. We bought Christmas cards and on December 13th we put up the Christmas tree and strung the lights but one was bad. He found the bad one. We often listened to the stereo while waiting for mail. We went over his assignments for therapy and watched the Lawrence Welk show. We practiced names of the week and month. On Sundays we go to church.

Walt helped clean the house and we shopped for groceries together. We wrapped Christmas gifts. We set up tables in the living room and practiced naming the house's objects. The family gathered at our house on December 21 and we ate food purchased from Kroger and opened gifts. He had a good day.

He wants to drive to the hospital and store so badly. His motor skills are good. We shall see about his reaction time first. We talked at length about his mother and dad's lives in order to write a history.

John came by on Christmas Day before joining his in-laws. We ate chili for lunch. It was a gray, gloomy day.

Editor's note: At this point, Emma ended her journal except for dates of upcoming medical appointments.

Walter's initial medical tests revealed hard stenosis of the right internal and left external carotid artery and blockage of up to 49 percent. His speech and language evaluation described "salad speech; I, lee, la, lo." He understood verbal communications when slow and simple. He exhibited the typical behaviors seen in people who are masking communication deficits; laughing, echolalia, rote responses such as "oh", "yes", that's it".

After a bout with pneumonia, Walter passed away in January 1998, which is also Emma's birthday. They shared over 56 years together.

Editor's note: The following letter was written by Emma over the course of several months after Walter's death. The words inside of brackets, however are not her words but added to clarify her narrative.

A Letter to Walter by Emma

Dearest,

I didn't expect you to die. I thought that you were improving, though slower than I anticipated. Even when you had your pneumonia, I assumed you would get better and you did. At least the lung specialist said so.

There were times when I felt a bit sorry for myself being so isolated during your illness, but it really wasn't so bad for I had you to talk with and care for. You had always been so willing to care for me.

Now I feel sorry for myself because I don't have you here to talk with and care for -- and all the tasks you did I now must do without your guidance. Thank you for teaching me so much about our finances etc. during the period of your illness. Thank you for leaving me in such good financial shape.

How much of your illness did you mask -- I was slow to learn of your hearing loss. I knew you had complained but I had no idea it was so great. Forgive me for not being aware. I wonder how much your low red blood count played in your last, short period of illness. Should we have done something about it?

Walter's Illness & Widowhood
By Emma

I hated the days you were in the hospital because you hated them so much. I really felt bad with my flu at the time, but I regret that I didn't stay all night when you wanted me to do so. I wonder if things might have been different if I had. You must have felt that the whole world was against you, and of course you wanted to do everything "your way".

I know you must have felt quite helpless when you were taking therapy I organized for you. It was a cruel joke for you to be robbed of your speech and your dignity. You did learn to mask your inability to say everything you wanted to say, however. I noticed you the last time we were in church together and you said not a word nor sang one note. How difficult that must have been!

Didn't we have a lovely Christmas? The children thought it was the best we had ever had. I wondered if you would be able to give out the gifts. You didn't miss a name, congratulations. We shall have to do it differently next Christmas. It will be hard for all of us. We shall feel your presence among us, however.

I wear your sweaters and shall use the money we received in a certificate on tours. I hope I won't have any difficulty. It will never be the same without you. I miss you most at church and on my walks. Everyone has rallied around and supported me. It still hurts!

Easter is coming up and I shall go worship with our children and grandchildren. We shall try to get together for Mother's Day here. Artie will pick up your Easter lily and put it on your grave. The nameplate is here. The children had one at Effingham and we brought it home with us.

Easter was comforting as I stayed with quiet, sturdy, understanding Debbie and Gary, and with Laura. Laura worries me. She is so sweet, but rebellious and with far too many privileges.

I spent one day with Kaye. We worked on redoing her curtains in the living room and she typed up lists, etc. for her book, which I wish we weren't making. We had a good day and a good night with both Kaye and Terry. We talked a bit about Bonnie and how she is maturing and getting her life together.

Saturday was Laura's birthday and we celebrated it with cake and ice cream. I can't believe she is 17.

Sunday, Deb went to church with me. She is uncomfortable in that church. I'm sorry! We met Kaye, Charlie, Justin, and Jennifer. Kathy sang in the choir and participated in the bell choir. After church Deb went home so Gary could go to his parents' and Laura went along. The rest of us went to Charlie's -- I rode out with Justin and had a good talk with him. Kaye and Terry, Kathy's mother and two sisters and their family were there. I was really tired from all the people and the activities -- food, egg hunt, gifts, etc.

Monday morning Charlie and Kathy picked me up at Debbie's and we came home. We stopped to eat lunch with John at the China Buffet. He seemed to like that.

Charlie tilled a place for flowers and herbs and Peggy brought me tomatoes, peppers, and basil plants. It rained a little but I planted them and some flower seeds. I shall hate to hoe the weeds when it gets hot. John had already mowed the lawn. It looked beautiful.

I took my first trip without you and found, as I expected, that it isn't nearly as much fun. I felt alone in all the group though all were kind. I shall take more trips and try again. When I arrived home tired, I wondered why I went.

Today I cleaned, sorted and pitched, planted herbs, flowers and fertilized, then mowed the west side of the house. A little shower and a hairdo helped my spirits.

Our nameplate is here and is in place at your gravesite. It looks very nice. It is like your parents, which I had cleaned, except more plain. I placed the "Circuit Rider" plate under your name. It is handsome there. Granddad's had to be set in cement above his name as we didn't want to have the bible and cross grandmother put on his nameplate to be covered or disturbed. We set a lily from the church service at Easter there. Kaye and Charlie had one in their church for you and I brought it home. We shall see if they will live.

John is around a good deal to mow the lawn, help me make decisions, record and carry out these decisions. He is so dependable. Deb calls each Sunday evening and comes every other week. I don't know how I could do without her.

I'm having a retina specialist look at my eye. I trust it is not hopeless. We said that we doubted it would be better, didn't we? I had a blood test for thyroid as the nurse and doctor at the dental clinic advised me to do so. I haven't heard any results.

I need to do something with my hair, but what? I drive to Mt. Vernon to the UMC meeting. I went the back way and stopped off at Laura and Bus' on the way home. Neither of them have good health. I'm feeling more adequate driving now. I'm a bit out of my "fog".

Carl is coming home. He has a new car like ours and so do Laura and Bus. Carl is driving and I hope makes it okay.

I visited Lil and gave her Jim's pictures. Then I visited Fred and Una (Duckworth). They are in poor health also. We're all getting old. Carl stayed here even after I took off for the UMW Assembly in Orlando. It was a good trip for me.

The chair you used so much when you were ill has been (re)*covered and looks nice.*

John, Kaye, and I went out to the cemetery this Memorial Day. They wanted to see our nameplate and say good-bye again. Guess what? A little tomato plant was growing on your grave. We all had a good laugh and wished we could protect it from the mower.

One day when Deb came unexpectedly, I wasn't home so she tried three places to find me, Kroger, Aldi, and the cemetery. Guess where she found me, the cemetery.

The Easter Lilies are living and looking good. The rest of the garden looks good. Kaye and Terry brought forsythia and at least one branch looks good.

Walter's Illness & Widowhood
By Emma

I hate to tell you that Laura is pregnant -- due Thanksgiving. She wants to keep her child. Deb and Gary and I are beside ourselves. I'd keep her here. They say "no". Kaye and Kathy and Charlie are helpful. I haven't told John yet, or is it my place? We shall all get through it. She is taking a College course.

Vera is helping me with Medicare (organizing bills). She is plotting it on business paper. The lady, Debbie, from the Clinic will call Wednesday to talk about that bill.

I go to Chicago finally on Thursday to Sunday. Bonnie has bought a house and I may stay over to help her move. Kaye and Terry bought a new house near Deb. They sold the old one immediately.

I have a neighborhood boy cutting the lawn each week. He only charges $8. I find it all I can handle with shrubs, trimming, fighting moles, a bit of water in the basement, etc. I don't enjoy keeping up the car either.

I still walk though usually only half the distance. I miss you along. I see the neighbors and we stop and talk.

Lyle Solverson died, as did John Turner, Dan Rollings, and Lloyd Barnard, but you know all this!

I started Sunday school. I sit with the preacher or Artie and Hope. It is getting easier, though still not easy. Deb comes and goes with me a lot. I appreciate it.

I forgot to tell you that Deb took me to her tax consultant. She is so good and it was painless. She only charged $25. We owed more federal tax and less Illinois tax. Thanks for your good records.

John and I took out a CD and bought AARP mutual funds, one at steady low interest and one is riskier but at high interest. I hope we did what is best. I gave each of the kids $5,000 for Mother's Day. You would have liked that.

I despise this hot humid weather, but am so very thankful for air conditioning and the fact that I can afford it and much more.

Thanks! I'm so glad we got our new car two years ago and you enjoyed it awhile. With good luck, I should not need another.

Editor's note: Emma continued to live in the house on Rod Lane for another seven years and then another thirteen years in a two-bedroom duplex just down the street on Sunset Lane. A notebook was found among Emma's documents that contained information about a reunion with the "Youth of Olney" from the 1940s and 50s. Emma reached out to nearly thirty people who were part of the Methodist Church's youth group she spoke so fondly of while Walter was the minister in Olney. Below are some of the correspondence and other documents, including the invitation from Emma to the youth group.

2005 Reunion of the Olney Youth

Dear 1945-50 Youth Group of the Methodist Church at Olney, IL:

Several of us have expressed a desire to get together after all of these years. Would you be interested? Have you suggestions and dates?

We have addresses for: David and Carolyn Jennings Hurley, Sam and Ralph Totten, Lavan Baylor, Boyd Wagner, Janet Garrett Tuttle, Lynn Harper, Anita Borche Webb, Joyce Petty Michels, Linda and Anna Beth Stanford, Barbara Campbell, and Pat and Dale Finley. Can you supply us with others?

Lovingly, Emma L. Smith

June 4, 2005

Dear Friends,

I'm sorry to be so long getting this letter to you. I was ill for a while and am now trying to get my house ready to sell. I plan to move into an apartment.

September 23, 2005 we shall gather in Olney. It will not be a good date for all of you, but one of the classes has a reunion the next day, so we chose this date.

Bring all of your pictures, (both) past and present (and) your remembrances and your jokes. If you have suggestions, write or call me.

I have heard from some of you. I shall give you more details later.

Emma L. Smith

July 26, 2005

Dear Friends,

Time is creeping up on us, in more ways than one. We hope to see you at the Olney, IL First U.M. Church on Friday, September 23 at noon until whenever. I'll have a small lunch (waiting for you) from noon until two.

You can spend the afternoon remembering, showing pictures, singing, etc. Be sure to bring spouses along!

Send me a childhood picture of yourself so we can guess who they are. Put names and addresses on the back and I shall return them. Please send pictures whether you can come or not. We want everyone included in remembering "the good old days". In the evening at 5:30 pm we shall have a dinner catered there at the church.

Motels are Super 8 and Holiday Inn. I find the best prices on the Internet. I still think like a preacher's wife.

I'm enclosing all of the names and addresses that I have attained. If you know any more call me or contact them yourselves.

I'm looking forward to seeing all of you and hearing your stories. We may even have to pop some corn.

Sincerely, Emma Smith

<u>Editor's note</u>: It appeared that some sixteen people, including some spouses and children, came to the Olney youth reunion. Pictures of the group and other candid shots show a relaxed and other times excited group. Included in the group photo are Bruce and Elizabeth Dean, Emma Smith, Linda Standford Peterson, Carey Westall, Ralph and Jennie Lynn Totten, Sam and Marilyn Totten, Lavon Baylor, Bob Novack, and Anna Beth and John Herzer. According to the caption, not pictured were "Wid", Willard Pauley, Kaye Smith Kimpling, and Joyce Petty Michels. Fourteen cards of regret were sent to Emma with nice, personal updates on them.

In 2018 at age 97, Emma moved from Carbondale to Effingham, which is where three of her children lived. She moved into an assisted living facility.

Effingham by Emma

December 2018

Dear Friends and Family,

This is just a note to update you about my new address. After returning from Florida this spring, I made the decision to move to Effingham in order to be nearer to three of my five children. Because of Doctor's advice and my children's concerns, regretfully I will not be returning to Florida.

In Effingham I'm happily living at The Glenwood Assisted Living Facility. I have a one-bedroom apartment furnished with my own belongings. It is a carefree environment that provides three meals a day, housekeeping, and laundry services. I often use a walker for stability; otherwise The Glenwood has handrails on both sides of the hallways. Often I take long walks along the interior halls for exercise. When weather permits, I go outside for walks using the sidewalks that encircle our buildings.

I have made several new friends here and there are various activities offered that I can participate in if I choose to. Just to name a few, there are daily exercise classes, occasional craft classes, Bingo, movies, and singers come in to entertain us. I play Dominoes most evenings with a group of friends. There is a hair salon and Sunday church services offered here as well. During inclement weather I can safely stay in at The Glenwood with all my needs met.

As most of you know, I have five children, four grandchildren, and seven great-grandchildren. Three of my five children -- Deb, Kaye, and Charlie -- live in the Effingham area. They visit often and drive me to church and appointments. My son John still lives in Carbondale and comes up monthly to visit. John often brings my only remaining sibling, Carl Lutes with him. My oldest son, Dave lives full-time in Avon Park, Florida, so I unfortunately don't see him as often. Dave travels to Illinois for the Lutes family reunions and the day after Thanksgiving Christmas party with our family. He and I talk on the phone when we are able to fit the time into our busy schedules, ha!

I hope that you have a Merry Christmas, Happy Holidays, and a healthy New Year!

Sincerely, Emma

Traveling and Camping Trips by Emma

In 1956, we ordered a fourteen-foot Comet camper trailer designed to sleep four. We planned to pick the trailer up from the factory in Kansas City as our family of seven traveled west on vacation. Walter and I slept on the rear bed with six-month old Debbie at our feet. Four-year old John (he was called Mark at that time) slept on the floor

Charlie, Emma, and the camper

and ten-year old Kaye slept on the converted dinette. Eight-year old Charlie (he was called Buddy at that time) and twelve-year old Dave slept in a pup tent set up outside. That was the first of many annual two and three week trips the family took traveling the U.S. each summer. In approximately 1975 we bought a twenty-foot Layton brand camper. It was much larger camper and some of our children were grown and not at home by then. We used it only a season or two before selling it. But, that wasn't the end of our travels.

What I remember most about our numerous trips into mountain country was the beauty of it all, the wild flowers, especially the ones that grew in the snow in the middle of summer and the fields of wild flowers covering the sides of the mountains beside the lovely alpine lakes. I enjoyed the nature hikes with an interpreter nature guide, the streams rushing down the mountainsides, the fresh, fresh air coming into our trailer windows at night, and the wholesome food we cooked up each day. When we were traveling, Deb would remind us that we needed to "live a little" each afternoon about 2:00 p.m. with a Dairy Queen ice cream cone.

During the late 1970s when the children were all out on their own we took several trips around the U.S. by car. Walter had taken a class on investing in the stock market. After a few years of reinvesting Walter suggested we use the profits from our investments to take a major trip each year. Driving became harder on Walter over the years and we were introduced to a husband and wife coordinated bus Tour Company, so we traveled with that group. During our retirement years, we traveled to California, Alaska, Nova Scotia and other parts of eastern Canada, three times to Hawaii, and to Europe several times.

Camping Trip Memories by Their Children

A few years after dad and mom bought their first camper, we used it on a trip to Canada. The Canadian border guards asked each of us where we were from and we all answered "Illinois" as best we could. We visited the Astrodome in Houston, the New York Fair, hiked in the Rockies and Sequoia National Parks. Most of our hikes were led by Park Rangers and nature guides who told us all about the sites we saw and sounds we heard.

We stood atop Pikes Peak and hiked underground into Carlsbad Caverns. At dusk one evening we sat and watched thousands of bats flying out of the caverns. The lights of Las Vegas shown down on us as we drove down the Vegas strip another evening.

Dad and mom always planned a stop at a Methodist Church for Sunday service no matter where we were. It may have been hot and the church not air-conditioned, but we dressed in our Sunday best in order to attend services as a fine, visiting family.

During long days travelling to far off camping areas we would often stop for a mid-afternoon treat. Usually led by little sister Debbie, she would utter her famous words of, "Isn't it time to stop and live a little?" which meant stop and eat ice cream at the next Dairy Queen as the days were hot and dusty if the A/C was not turned on.

To pass the time on long days of driving, we would often play games such as "how many miles to the top of the next hill" and "how many different state licenses plates can you spot?"

When not in use, the camper was often parked under a lean-to on granddad's farm. We remember going out to the farm and hearing granddad holler to the cows, "sooot, sooot, sooot," or some such uttering. We were told to watch were we stepped as cow pies were prevalent. "You'd sooner cut your foot than step on that!" granddad would warn us.

First Flu Shot by Emma

In about 1976 the first Swine Flu shots became available to the public. Walter's mother enlisted me to take her and we both received this immunization. The shots were given out in a public place such as a grocery store or bank. This was my first flu shot and I have gotten one every year since.

January 1966 School Trip by Emma

I remember being a lady sponsor with Vi Hankla, at our own expense, of high school girls for a trip to New York City and Washington D.C. Earl Renshaw and Boyd Wagner were the sponsors of the boys. We went by bus. It took all day to get there. We went to New York first. Each of us had our groups of both boys and ladies that we took around the City. After we visited one session of the United Nations together, our group wanted to go to Rockefeller Center. It was interesting finding the kind of food they wanted and to see the things in the City they wished to see in the small amount of time we had there and catch the last bus running back to our hotel.

We travelled by our bus to Washington, D.C. There was a huge snow storm and we were the last bus to get to Washington on the Interstate for there was so much snow that they shut it down behind us.

Needless to say, much of Washington was shut down the next day including the Congressional dining room where we had intended to eat because the workers could not get to work.

We did see and interview our Senators and Representatives. They were very courteous to us and answered our questions. I was quite aggravated at one of the youth who persisted in talking to others and eating candy during the question and answer period. Most of the youth were quite well behaved. They were glad to be there.

We stayed downtown in an old hotel. We had one whole floor to ourselves and the elevator attendant was instructed to let no one off at that floor except our youth with a sponsor. In the middle of the night there was a commotion and we later learned that a man had gotten onto that floor supposedly by mistake, and the hotel manager chased him down and evicted him. The girls had two large rooms and Vi and I had another. After the incident with the man on our floor, the girls took pillows and blankets and all slept in one room.

The trip home was uneventful though brutal for it was done at night. Some slept on the bus ride, I never could. I was not asked, nor did I volunteer to go again though the whole of it was a delightful trip and I'm glad I went once.

Many years later, when I ran across the list of names of the youth who went with us, I found a fellow in our church and a lady friend whose daughter and son-in-law went on the trip.

Postcard from Emma While in New York the During School Trip

We really took a good tour here. We must come back again. We go to the Broadway play "Skyscraper" tonight. Saw snow on Pennsylvania Mountains last night. Mother

David Smith by Emma

David was a handful. He was smarter than others were. He outsmarted us more than once. Grandpa Lutes once said, "That boy's going to end up in the penitentiary." I can still hear him saying that.

Carl was playing the flute and David knocked it out of Carl's hands. Carl said patiently, "Now Dave, don't do that. It's a precious instrument and costs a lot of money. It's made of silver." David would say OK. When Carl went back to playing away, David would swipe at it again. Carl waited for me, David's mother, to say something. When I didn't, Carl grabbed David up and spanked his bottom hard. I gave Carl a look as if to say, "How dare you! That's my child."

I should have spanked David more often I suppose. He was very hard to figure out how to deal with. As the first child, he had no older siblings to show him what to do. Then when Kaye came along, the two of them together... (<u>ed. note</u>: she never finished this sentence.)

Thoughts on Growing Older by Emma

What does it feel like to get old? It doesn't feel good!

After falling several times when I missed a step, one needs to be aware any way one can of steps -- look down and count. All steps should be stripped on the edge.

One has to watch one's steps on uneven ground. It is so much more fun to just step out wherever one is. One's steps become slower from fear of falling and lack of energy. One feels a lack of power because of these limited physical abilities.

Having never been able to think on the minute (ed. note: think quickly), it becomes even slower. After mulling it over I can think through it.

When one's eyes dim with age one sees more slowly, so the reading process is slowed down, including TV watching.

Editor's note: The following are random thoughts that were written but not explained in detail.

Physical, mental ability to do...

Good time honey, sweetie, Miss Emma (ed. note: we assume she dislikes these)

Survivor, wear flat shoes, longer sleeves...

Helpless, weak, not able, frustrating, moldering...

Hair color, skin, wrinkles, tire easily...

Naps, strength, grandchildren, eyes, up, down, bend over, walk, garden, housework...

Songs

Great Is Thy Faithfulness
For The Beauty of the Earth
Amazing Grace
Joyful, Joyful We Adore Thee
In the Bud There Is a Flower

Emma is on the Left

Editor's note: The following are Bible verses as interpreted and written by Emma.

Bible Verses

Isaiah 40:30-31 -- They that wait on the Lord shall renew their strength. They will soar on wings like eagles. They will run and not grow weary. They will walk and not be faint.

Micah 6:8 -- What does the Lord require of you? Act justly, love mercifully, and walk humbly with your God.

Hate what is evil, cling to what is good. Be joyful in hope, patient in affection, and faithful in prayer. Do not be overcome by evil, but overcome evil with good.

Trust in the Lord with all your heart and lean not on thine own understanding. In all thy ways acknowledge Him and He will direct thy path.

All things work together for good for those who love God, to those who are called for His purpose.

For God so loved the world that He gave His only beloved son that whosoever believeth in Him shall be saved.

This is the day the Lord hath made, let us rejoice and be glad in it.

Psalms -- Make a joyful noise unto the Lord all ye lands. Serve the Lord with gladness. Come before His presence with singing. Know ye that the Lord is God. It is He that hath made us and not we ourselves. We are His people and the sheep of His pasture. Be thankful unto Him and bless His name for His truth endureth forever and His mercy unto all generations.

Psalms 23 -- The Lord is my Shepherd.

I believe in the sun when it does not shine, I believe in God when He is silent.

Romans 5:3-5 -- We can rejoice in our sufferings knowing that suffering produces character, character produces patience and hope, and hope does not disappoint us.

Thespians 5:16-18 -- Rejoice evermore. Pray without ceasing. In everything give thanks, for this is the will of God in Christ Jesus concerning you.

Thespians 5:18 -- Give thanks in all circumstances

Philistines 1:21 -- For to me, to live is Christ and to die is gain

Philistines 3:13-14 -- This one thing I do, forgetting what lies behind and straining forward to what lies ahead, I press on toward the goal for the prize of the heavenly call of God in Christ Jesus.

Bless the Lord, oh my soul, and forget not all His benefits, who forgives all of your inequities, who heals all your diseases, who redeems your life from the pit, who crowns you with steadfast love and mercy, who surrounds you with love for as long as you shall live.

Hebrews 12:14 -- Follow peace with all men and holiness without which no man shall see the Lord.

Sayings

T. H. Thompson, John Watson -- "Be kinder than necessary, for everyone you meet is fighting some kind of battle."

Inside the Parish Fence by Emma

We often hear gripes about raising children "inside the parish fence." They do live in a glass house. When I think of parsonage children this story comes to mind.

Her Favorites
By Emma

A minister's son was in a Sunday school class where the teacher was trying to get the children to join the church on Easter. The PK, or preacher's kid, said, "I'm not joining this church because as soon as my dad finishes his schooling, we're pulling out of here." Perhaps we bring trouble upon ourselves by talking too much in front of our children.

But, the joy of raising children inside the parish fence far outweighs the negative. If our "wee ones" can't see grandmother as often as they like, there is a whole church full of grandmothers who shower their love on our kids.

When our babies are born, they belong not just to us, but to the whole congregation who are interested in their rapid growth and development. I think just now of the little girl who broke her leg while both parents were away. With typical Methodist organization, a loving constant vigil was set up beside that bed, 24-hours each day until the parents returned.

Let's think of the many parish ladies who borrow parsonage children at just the time when the mother needs a rest from them. Let's think of the congregation rejoicing when gladness comes into our children's lives and sympathy in times of sorrow. Good grades made the whole congregation proud.

What about the fence? With more ministers' children in the book of "Who's Who" perhaps the fence helps to discipline them to life. When a son decides on his own that the basketball shoes he moved with him were given to him by the coach, and he cleans them and sends them back, or when a child on his own raises his church giving in accordance to his job and allowance, or when a six year old on layman's day tells her daddy, "It took five men to be as good as you are," or when a daughter walks down the aisle alone in front of the whole Sunday morning congregation to present herself in Christian work.

This is when a minister's wife realizes the boundless joy of raising children "inside the parish fence."

Benedictions
By Walter

Editor's note: The following benedictions were found among Walter's papers.

Benedictions by Walter

Let us pray! And now may the God of faithfulness and peace encourage all of you to heed both what you have heard and felt in this hour of corporate worship. May you live in harmony and accord both with Christ and with each other every day of the coming week. And may the blessing of God Almighty, Father, Son, and Holy Spirit be with you. Amen.

Let us pray! Let us remember the promise of our Lord that where two or three are gathered together in His name He is present. May we recognize His presence here, rejoice in His blessings, and lift up our hearts in thanksgiving. Dismiss us now, O Lord, and accompany us on every pathway our feet shall take in the week ahead, that we may live in peace and love and holiness through the blessing of God Almighty, Father, Son, and Holy Spirit. Amen.

Let us pray! We have met here, O lord God, to offer unto you honor and glory and praise. You are the God of hope. Through your grace may hope abound in all of us. Comfort our hearts with your eternal blessings and establish us in peace, through Jesus Christ your son. Amen.

Let us pray! O God, our Father, grant that we may remember what our ears have heard, what our lips have spoken, what our hearts have experienced in your house today. May we truly believe in our hearts and practice in our daily lives those holy precepts and teachings that you have made known to us today. May the Blessings of God Almighty, Father, Son, and Holy Spirit be with you. Amen.

Let us pray! And now may the God of steadfast love and encouragement grant you leave to live in harmony with each other and in full accord with Christ our Lord, that together we may all with one voice glorify God our Father and serve Him daily with our lives. May the blessing of God Almighty, Father, Son, and Holy Spirit be with you. Amen.

<u>Editor's Note</u>: The following sermon was given by Walter A. Smith on June 29, 1977 at the Southeast District Summer Bible Conference at Lake Swan Camp in Melrose, Florida. This transcript was made from an audio cassette tape of the event using voice recognition software.

The Mystery of Angels by Walter

My subject for this evening is "The Mystery of Angels." I think it was the second night of camp meeting when I saw Harley and I announced to him my subject and asked for this order of worship. And, would you believe it? Two of our four camp meeting preachers stole my thunder.

Walter Smith

The Mystery of Angels - Hear these words of Scripture.

"Now there were in the same country shepherds abiding in the field, keeping watch over their flock by night. And behold an angel of the Lord appeared before them and the glory of the Lord shown round about them. And they were greatly afraid.

"Then the angel said to them 'Do not be afraid. For behold I bring you good tidings of great joy, which shall be to all people. For there is born to you this day in the City of David a Savior who is Christ the Lord. And this will be a sign to you. You will find the babe wrapped in swaddling clothes and lying in a manger.' And suddenly there was with the angel a multitude of the heavenly host, praising God and saying, 'Glory to God in the highest, and on Earth peace, goodwill toward men.'

"So it was, when the angels were gone away into heaven, the shepherds said one to another, 'Let us now go to Bethlehem and see this thing that has come to pass, which the Lord has made known unto us.'"

Then just a brief word from the end of the life of our Lord:

The Mystery of Angels
By Walter

"Now after the end of the Sabbath, towards the first day of the week, Mary Magdalene and the other Mary came to see the tomb and behold there was a great earthquake, for an angel of the Lord descended and came and rolled back the stone and sat up on it. His countenance was like lightning, and his clothing as white as the snow, and the guard shook for fear of him and became like dead men.

"But the angel answered and said to the women, 'Do not be afraid. For I know that you seek Jesus who was crucified. He is not here. He has risen as he said. Come see the place where the Lord lay and go quickly and tell his disciples that he has risen. And indeed he is going before you into Galilee. You will see him there.'

"So they departed quickly from the tomb with fear and great joy and ran to bring the disciples the word."

Here are two stories, one from the beginning of the Ministry of our Lord and the other for the end of his earthly life. There's a common thread among them, its angels and their message. These angels are mysterious messengers of the miracle of birth and the miracle of the resurrection.

One Sunday about four years ago, our pastor at home mentioned angels in his sermon. He indicated that he believed in them. On leaving church I asked him, have you ever preached a sermon on angels? And he said no I haven't. And I said why not? He said I guess I just don't know enough about them.

I began thinking about them myself. Almost 40 years I've held license to preach and not once in those 40 years have I ever preached a sermon on angels. My excuse is like his, I don't know enough about them.

Angelology is very trendy today. We meet it everywhere, even at camp meeting. In the marketplace angels are especially prevalent. There are angel magazines. There are angel cookbooks. There's angel perfume. There's angel pasta. There's angel water. There's angel pins. There are angel earrings, and on and on I could go.

A recent Gallup poll indicates that about 72 percent of the American people believe in angels. That's a little strange because we are all products of the age of science. I know I am, and I want proof.

The Mystery of Angels
By Walter

I've never seen an angel. I've never heard an angel. I've never touched an angel. Can you tell me what an angel tastes like? Can you tell me what an angel smells like? I want some proof, some scientific proof.

Such a desire for physical proof misses the point completely. I am told that angels are mentioned in the Bible over 700 times. Would you believe that?

I took a little look through the Hymnal. I think there must be at least 200 Hymns in our own Hymnal that mentions angels or the heavenly house or in some way refers to these spiritual beings.

Anything referred to so often in the Scriptures ought to at least cause us to ponder a while. And yet I never preached a sermon on angels. And the excuse I gave is I don't know enough about them. Angels are so flimsy. They're so silky. They're so cloudy. They're there and they're gone. They're so mysterious.

Ancient mankind didn't have this trouble that I have. Especially in the Near East they'd go out on the house tops and look up at the stars and ponder. To them every star represented an angel. There were guiding stars and guiding angels. There were guarding stars and guarding angels. It was easy to believe in angels then.

The Bible characters also, both in the Old and the New Testament, meet angels especially at times of crisis in their lives. The life of Christ is an excellent example. There were angels at his birth, lots of them. Mary had an angel visitant. Joseph had an angel visitant. Elizabeth had an angel visitant. The shepherds had an angel visitant. There were angels in Gethsemane, at the resurrection, at the ascension. Many other Bible characters have witnessed to having seen angels and heard their message; scores of them too many to mention here.

And still I shrink back. I'm reluctant. Why am I so reluctant? Well if I told you that I saw an angel on the way to church tonight you'd start tapping your heads. Don't tell me you wouldn't? You'd say he's gone loco on us. I've never had any personal contact with an angel. In fact, I know so little about them that I ought to be very careful of what I say.

You ask me, do you believe in angels? I say, sometimes, but sometimes no. Angels are very vague to me. And yet the Scriptures force me to think about them seriously.

The Mystery of Angels
By Walter

There are about three questions that I like to mention just briefly. First, what is an angel?

My first response is it's a symbol of perfection and innocence. An angel signifies purity and holiness and sanctity. We say that someone has an angelic expression on his face. We mean he appears to be completely innocent. On the other hand, I've been accused of some misdoing or sin and I respond I'm no angel! Don't expect me to be perfect.

When asked, what is an angel? I would say on a more serious side, an angel is a creature of God, a creation of God just like you and I are. God made them a little less than himself, according to the Scriptures, and a little more than mankind. Angels are pure spirits with no material bodies. They must have some kind of body because they appear and then they disappear. Is it a glorified body like the one that Jesus had after the resurrection?

Since it's so hard to see an angel and to comprehend what he is like, we ask, do the angels have halos over their hands? Do they have wings sprouting from their shoulders? Do they wear a white robe?

All of these things miss the point. Angels are a symbol of doing God's will perfectly. They always do God's will. We do not. They are perfect. We are not. They constantly praise God. We do not.

Many Scriptures declare the reality of angels, and those who have seen them testify that they are very real. Take the story of Jacob, when he wrestled with an angel all night and went away limping ever after, the rest of his life, after his encounter with an angel.

Once gone, they can never be called back. Angels never die. So we assume that they are still present though invisible. Anyone who has ever experienced an angel, according to the Scriptures, will never forget it. It is an unforgettable experience. You ponder it over and over again. And that leads me to ask, what is an angel? It's a mystery to most of us.

Secondly I'd like to ask, where do angels live? Where do they dwell?

Some scholars believe that there is an upper cosmos God created especially for angels just like he created the earth for us. But this is so remote and is not mentioned in the Bible. I pass it by.

The Mystery of Angels
By Walter

At this point I am guided by the Lord's Prayer. You say what? The Lord's Prayer has a lot to say about it. Where do angels live? "Our Father," we say, "Who art in heaven" seems to suggest that heaven is a place and God lives there and angels live there. If we believe in heaven, it ought to be easy to believe in angels. And we continue to pray, "Thy will be done, on earth as it is in heaven." A place created by God, just as He created the earth.

Where is heaven? I can't find it on a map. What direction is it? I don't know whether it's up or down or east or west. But I believe in heaven as a place created by God, where He rules supremely.

The last question that I want to ask is what do angels do? What is their mission?

They are messengers of God, always ready to do God's will. A good example of this is the Annunciation, where an angel appeared to Mary and said, "Mary, favored one, you have found favor with God. Do not be afraid. You will bear a son. Call his name Jesus."

Messenger is what an angel is, a messenger of peace and comfort and fulfillment. These messengers remind us that God is everywhere. That he can speak to us at any moment.

And more, they lead us in the worship of God. The Scriptures often tell of angels leading us to praise God. Take Isaiah six, "In the year that King Isaiah died, I saw the Lord. And his train filled the temple. And the Seraphim were crying Holy, Holy, Holy is the lord of hosts." This is great instruction on how to worship God.

Angels do more. They testified to the supremacy of God. We hear about the hosts of heaven, the armies of God. How many are there? Was it Daniel who said there are ten thousand times ten thousand? The point is there are countless hosts suggesting that God will never be defeated. The armies of heaven will always win.

Luther wrote a hymn about this. He said, "The Prince of Darkness grim. We tremble not for him. His rage we can endure for lo his doom is sure. One little word shall fell him."

Angels are a symbol of doxology. The doxology goes beyond ordinary worship. Listen to it. "Praise God from whom all blessings flow. Praise him all creatures here below. Praise him above yea heavenly hosts. Praise father, son, and Holy Ghost." This worship rises above our earthly realm. The hosts of heaven lead us and lift us beyond ourselves and all human expression. Yes, angels lead us in praise of God. What a glorious thought.

In conclusion I would like to ask, would you like to meet an angel? You asked me, would I like to meet an angel? It is so popular a fad as if meeting an angel is desirable.

They say that angels are all about us. Some testimonies of angels I believe in, as when a person who is close to death. You have heard these stories. I remember when I was in the eighth grade. I used to go with my father on calls, when he went out to visit his parishioners. I remember one day he took us to the home of our Sunday school superintendent who was dying of cancer. As a matter of fact, when we walked into the room he was in a coma.

But dad spoke to him, "Brother Johnson." And he responded, immediately wide awake. And dad said, "How is everything?" He said, "I've seen the other side. It's all right." I have no doubt in my mind that the man had seen an angel, the spirit of God, call it whatever you want; he saw him clearly, and all was alright.

All of us may experience times of crisis in our lives when deep inside us there is an assurance that God's with us. No white winged angel came. Down inside, there was an inner witness that all is well, the forces of the enemies will be defeated and we shall experience triumph forever.

Would you like to meet an angel? Would you believe that Martin Luther, the great reformer, prayed that he would never see an angel? He thought the experience was too awesome for these frail lives of ours. He might have heart failure. It might drive him crazy. He might have a seizure. I tend to agree.

A favorite hymn of mine says, "I asked no dream, no prophet ecstasy, no sudden rending of the veil of clay, no angel visitant, no opening skies. But God take the dimness of my soul away." I want to be sensitive to the heavenly presence in my life and I hope that you will be. But I don't care whether I ever meet an angel or not.

Still, the richness of meeting Christ and his marvelous Grace empties my soul from any desire of wanting to see anything more than He. A Gospel song puts it well. Speaking of angels, "And when they hear salvation story they will fold their wings, for angels never felt the joy that our salvation brings."

Here's another way of looking at angels. All of us in our congregations have met devout people who quietly testified every day to the providence of God's love in their lives. They live very close to God, they walk close to Him and when they were gone we've been forced to say, truly an angel was in our midst.

We are reminded of the time when those three messengers came to Abraham and Sarah. In the course of the evening meals they told Abraham that they would have a son, and Sarah laughed. And when they were gone, Abraham chided Sarah and said to her, we have entertained angels unawares. We need to be more sensitive to God's messengers. It may be that we too entertain angels unaware.

Human life, being that it is a disturbing mixture of good and evil, is still a medium through which we might meet an angel if we were sensitive to God's presence. You ask me again, would you like to meet an angel? And I say if I could stand it. I don't know whether I could or not. I'd rather be an angel than meet one, wouldn't you?

To bring hope to somebody, that's angelic. To bring fulfillment to others, that's angelic. To bring peace and joy to others, that's angelic. If I could lead one wandering soul to find God, that would be the work of an angel.

In the process, God and angels become real to me. I hope they do to you.

To Dave, Kaye, Charlie, John and Deb by Emma

Dear Children,

Thanks for the "roast" at my 90th Birthday Party. It was unexpected and fun. I was so surprised that I could not even say a decent "thank you."

I hope you realize how dear you all are to me. Each of you have unique qualities all your own and I appreciate them.

There was a day when I wished to send some or all of you back where you came from, but never could figure out where to

Emma & Walter Smith, 1941

send you. Now I don't know how I could bear to live without you. You have been so kind and so and so thoughtful to me that I feel truly blessed.

You understood and tolerated my "little" quirks and eccentricities and interpreted my love in such a way that it made my life a joy to be among you.

Thank you for understanding each other's fine, as well as less than fine points, loving and forgiving each other and me, so that you were all five best friends. Your trips together attested to that. I am very proud of you all. When crisis comes, you all five rallied around and I could depend on you.

I am glad God gave you to me. I have come to rely upon you, maybe too much. Always remember, I love you!

From Mom

Printed in the United States
By Bookmasters